Hometown
COOKING.

Volume 4
Meredith® Consumer Marketing
Des Moines, Iowa

Family Circle® Hometown Cooking

Meredith® Corporation Consumer Marketing
Vice President, Consumer Marketing: David Ball
Consumer Product Marketing Director: Steve Swanson
Consumer Marketing Product Manager: Wendy Merical
Business Director: Ron Clingman
Associate Director, Production: Al Rodruck

Waterbury Publications, Inc.
Contributing Project Editor and Writer: Liz Woolever, Spectrum
    Communication Services, Inc.
Editorial Director: Lisa Kingsley
Associate Editor: Tricia Laning
Creative Director: Ken Carlson
Associate Design Director: Doug Samuelson
Production Assistant: Mindy Samuelson
Contributing Copy Editors: Terri Fredrickson, Gretchen Kauffman, Peg Smith
Contributing Indexer: Elizabeth T. Parson

Family Circle® **Magazine**
Editor in Chief: Linda Fears
Creative Director: Karmen Lizzul
Food Director: Regina Ragone, M.S., R.D.
Senior Food Editor: Julie Miltenberger
Associate Food Editor: Michael Tyrrell

Meredith Publishing Group
President: Tom Harty
Executive Vice President: Andy Sareyan
Vice President, Manufacturing: Bruce Heston

Meredith Corporation
President and Chief Executive Officer: Stephen M. Lacy

In Memoriam: E.T. Meredith III (1933–2003)

Pictured on the front cover:
Whoopie Pie Treats
(recipe on page 172)
Photography by Scott Little

Enjoy prizewinning recipes from hometown America!

If you enjoy cooking, winning a blue ribbon or capturing first place in a recipe contest is as good as it gets. Striving for that is what keeps competitive cooks in the kitchen trying a little of this and a pinch of that, and making dishes over and over in search of the perfect result. Now, with the sensational ideas in *Family Circle® Hometown Cooking* Volume 4, you can sample the very best recipes from America's hometown cooks.

We've gathered the most popular recipes from community cookbooks and cooking competitions all across the country into one eye-catching collection. There are more than 150 recipes for you to try, including 30-minute meals, mouthwatering breakfasts, sensational sandwiches and pizzas, good-for-you meals, potluck favorites, ideas for the grill, as well as irresistible desserts. All are designed to please families and keep the tradition of sharing great home-cooked food alive. As you explore the book, you'll meet some of the cooks who perfected these dishes and learn the secrets behind their prizewinning specialties. So don't waste a minute; check out these terrific recipes now. You'll be glad you did!

— The Editors

TABLE OF
CONTENTS

Getting Started   6

Bring On Breakfast   28

Meals in Minutes   50

Cook It Slowly   72

Great Grilling   92

Healthy Favorites   112

Potluck Pleasers   128

Handheld Favorites   150

Sweet Endings   166

Index   187

Chapter 1

GETTING STARTED

Get the party rolling with a selection of these tantalizing appetizers.

Cheese-Stuffed Jalapeños

DIPS AND SPREADS

Arugula Pesto Dip, 8

Blue Cheese Ball, 14

Cheddar-Thyme Sweet
Onion Dip, 11

Chèvre and
Tomato Spread, 8

Cranberry-
Pistachio Pâté, 12

Fresh Onion Dip, 11

DRINKS

Champagne Punch, 15

Hot Cranberry Punch, 14

HOT APPETIZERS

Bacon and Gorgonzola
Cornbread Sliders with
Chipotle Mayo, 17

Bite-Size Chicken
Empanadas, 18

Bourbon-Molasses-Glazed
Chicken Wings, 20

Brie-Pecan Quesadillas, 20

Cheese-Stuffed
Jalapeños, 26

Ladder Loaf with Roasted
Pepper Filling, 19

Mexican Meatballs, 22

Tomato Quiche Tartlets, 22

Vidalia Sweetest
Onion-Licious Pie, 25

Warm Brie, 12

COLD APPETIZERS

Tequila-Marinated
Shrimp, 26

NUTS AND SNACK MIX

Toasted Almonds
with Rosemary and
Cayenne, 27

Arugula Pesto Dip

Arugula is a wonderful peppery alternate for basil in this pesto. Thoroughly dry the leaves before pureeing the mixture in the blender.

MAKES 1 cup **START TO FINISH** 30 minutes

1½	cups fresh parsley leaves
1	cup arugula leaves (2 ounces)
½	cup olive oil
⅓	cup pine nuts, toasted
¼	cup freshly grated Parmesan cheese
2	tablespoons lemon juice
¼	teaspoon salt
	Assorted vegetable dippers (such as Belgian endive leaves, radishes, asparagus spears, yellow sweet pepper strips, and carrot sticks)

① In a blender combine parsley, arugula, oil, pine nuts, Parmesan cheese, lemon juice, and salt. Cover and blend until smooth, scraping down sides with a rubber spatula as needed. Serve with assorted vegetables.

Make-Ahead Directions: Prepare as directed. Transfer mixture to an airtight container. Cover and store in the refrigerator for up to 3 days. Let stand at room temperature for 1 hour before serving. Serve with assorted vegetables.

PER 1 TABLESPOON DIP 85 calories; 9 g total fat (2 g sat. fat); 1 mg cholesterol; 67 mg sodium; 1 g carbohydrate; 1 g fiber; 2 g protein

Chèvre and Tomato Spread

Goat cheese, with its intense flavor, is a delightful complement to dried tomatoes and fresh basil. Together, they make an ideal spread for entertaining or everyday snacking.

MAKES 1¼ cups spread **PREP** 20 minutes **CHILL** 2 to 4 hours

---

	Boiling water
⅓	cup dried tomatoes (not oil pack)
4	ounces soft goat cheese (chèvre)
½	of an 8-ounce package reduced-fat cream cheese (Neufchâtel), softened
¼	cup snipped fresh basil or 2 teaspoons dried basil, crushed
3	cloves garlic, minced
⅛	teaspoon black pepper
1	to 2 tablespoons milk
10	slices party rye bread or 20 assorted reduced-fat crackers
	Assorted garnishes (such as halved or quartered cherry tomatoes, broccoli florets, chopped yellow sweet pepper, and/or small fresh basil leaves) (optional)

① In a small bowl pour enough boiling water over dried tomatoes to cover. Let stand for 10 minutes. Drain tomatoes, discarding liquid. Finely snip tomatoes.

② In a medium bowl stir together the snipped tomatoes, goat cheese, cream cheese, snipped fresh or dried basil, garlic, and black pepper. Stir in enough of the milk to make mixture of spreading consistency. Cover and chill for 2 to 4 hours. Serve with rye bread or crackers. If desired, top with assorted garnishes.

PER 2 TABLESPOONS SPREAD 92 calories; 5 g total fat (3 g sat. fat); 13 mg cholesterol; 188 mg sodium; 7 g carbohydrate; 1 g fiber; 5 g protein

Chèvre and Tomato Spread

Fresh Onion Dip

Fresh Onion Dip

Go wild with dippers! Start with these ideas and then branch out to cooked or raw vegetables, such as potatoes, sweet potatoes, beets, green beans, cucumber, wax beans, radishes, daikon, and baby carrots, plus assorted crackers and chips.

MAKES 1½ cups **PREP** 15 minutes **COOK** 5 minutes
CHILL 1 to 24 hours

———————◆———————

1½ cups chopped sweet onion (such as Vidalia or Walla Walla)
2 tablespoons butter or margarine
1 8-ounce carton sour cream
¼ teaspoon salt
¼ teaspoon coarsely ground black pepper
⅛ teaspoon cayenne pepper
   Milk (optional)
4 teaspoons snipped fresh chives
   Assorted dippers (such as chips, crackers, and/or vegetable dippers)

① In a medium skillet cook onion in hot butter about 5 minutes or until tender. Cool.

② In a blender or food processor combine cooked onion, sour cream, salt, black pepper, and cayenne pepper. Cover and blend or process until nearly smooth.

③ Transfer to a small bowl. Cover and chill for 1 to 24 hours.

④ Before serving, stir in additional milk, 1 teaspoon at a time, if necessary to make dipping consistency; sprinkle with chives. Serve with assorted dippers.

PER 1 TABLESPOON DIP 33 calories; 3 g total fat (1 g sat. fat); 7 mg cholesterol; 41 mg sodium; 1 g carbohydrate; 0 g fiber; 0 g protein

Cheddar-Thyme Sweet Onion Dip

A blend of three cheeses adds both creaminess and flavor to this warm dip.

MAKES 16 servings **PREP** 25 minutes
BAKE 30 minutes **OVEN** 375°F

———————◆———————

1 large sweet onion (such as Vidalia or Maui), finely chopped (3 cups)
6 ounces Monterey Jack cheese with jalapeños, shredded (1½ cups)
6 ounces reduced-fat cheddar cheese, shredded (1½ cups)
4 ounces light cream cheese
½ cup light mayonnaise
1 teaspoon snipped fresh thyme or ¼ teaspoon dried thyme, crushed
   Crackers or toast

① Preheat oven to 375°F. Place 2 cups of the onion in a large bowl. In a food processor combine the remaining onion, the shredded cheeses, cream cheese, mayonnaise, and thyme. Cover and process until nearly smooth; stir into onion in bowl. Spoon into a shallow 1½-quart baking dish.

② Bake for 20 minutes. Stir. Bake for 10 minutes more. Cool slightly before serving. Serve with crackers or toast.

PER SERVING 127 calories; 10 g total fat (5 g sat. fat); 23 mg cholesterol; 158 mg sodium; 4 g carbohydrate; 1 g fiber; 7 g protein

Warm Brie

This spread deserves a place on your next appetizer buffet. It's impressive, simple to prepare, and, best of all, YUMMY!

MAKES 8 servings **START TO FINISH** 20 minutes **OVEN** 350°F

- 1   8-ounce round Brie cheese
- ¼   cup butter or margarine
- ¼   cup packed brown sugar
- ¼   cup chopped nuts
- 1   tablespoon honey

① Preheat oven to 350°F. Place round of Brie in a shallow baking dish or pie plate. Bake for 10 minutes.

② Meanwhile, in a small saucepan combine butter, brown sugar, nuts, and honey. Bring to boiling on medium heat, stirring constantly. Pour sauce over Brie. To serve, cut into wedges.

PER SERVING 201 calories; 16 g total fat (8 g sat. fat); 43 mg cholesterol; 246 mg sodium; 10 g carbohydrate; 0 g fiber; 6 g protein

Cranberry-Pistachio Pâté

Serve this country-style beef, pork, cranberry, and pistachio nut pâté with cornichons and/or toasted baguette rounds.

MAKES 24 servings **PREP** 30 minutes
BAKE 1½ hours **CHILL** 8 to 24 hours **OVEN** 350°F

- Nonstick cooking spray
- 1   egg
- ¾   cup dried cranberries
- ½   cup chopped shallots or onion
- ½   cup chopped pistachio nuts
- ⅓   cup port wine or cranberry juice
- ¼   cup half-and-half or light cream
- ¼   cup fine dry bread crumbs
- 2   teaspoons dried sage leaves, crushed, or ½ teaspoon ground sage
- 1   teaspoon salt
- 1   teaspoon coarsely ground black pepper
- 2   cloves garlic, minced
- 1   pound lean ground beef
- 1   pound lean ground pork
- Stone-ground mustard

① Preheat oven to 350°F. Lightly coat a 9 x 5 x 3-inch loaf pan with cooking spray; set aside.

② In a large bowl beat egg. Add cranberries, shallots, pistachio nuts, port wine or cranberry juice, cream, bread crumbs, sage, salt, pepper, and garlic; mix well. Add ground beef and pork. Use clean hands to mix well. Press mixture into prepared pan. Cover tightly with foil. Bake for 1½ hours.

③ Remove pan from oven. Cool slightly. Uncover; carefully pour off drippings, leaving pâté in pan. Cover pâté loosely with foil. Place several heavy cans of food (to serve as weights) in another 9 x 5 x 3-inch loaf pan. Place pan with weights on top of the covered pâté. Chill for 8 to 24 hours.

④ Remove weighted pan and foil. Loosen sides if necessary. Invert pâté onto a serving platter. Cut pâté in half lengthwise; cut into thin slices. Serve with stone-ground mustard.

Make-Ahead Directions: Prepare as directed, except after removing pâté from pan, wrap pâté in plastic wrap and store in the refrigerator for up to 2 days.

PER SERVING 97 calories; 5 g total fat (2 g sat. fat); 31 mg cholesterol; 138 mg sodium; 6 g carbohydrate; 1 g fiber; 7 g protein

Cranberry-Pistachio Pâté

Blue Cheese Ball

Toasting the nuts for this creamy cheese ball boosts the wonderful nut flavor.

MAKES 2½ cups spread **PREP** 20 minutes **CHILL** 4 hours

- 2 8-ounce packages cream cheese, softened
- 1 4-ounce package crumbled blue cheese (1 cup)
- 1 teaspoon garlic powder
- ¼ teaspoon Worcestershire-style marinade for chicken
-    Dash bottled hot pepper sauce
- ½ cup chopped walnuts or pecans, toasted
-    Assorted crackers

① In a large bowl combine cream cheese, blue cheese, garlic powder, Worcestershire-style marinade, and hot pepper sauce. Beat with an electric mixer on low to medium until well mixed. Cover and chill about 4 hours or until firm enough to handle.

② Shape cheese mixture into a ball or log. Roll in nuts to coat. Serve immediately or store, covered, in the refrigerator for up to 24 hours. Serve with crackers.

PER 2 TABLESPOONS SPREAD 118 calories; 11 g total fat (6 g sat. fat); 29 mg cholesterol; 147 mg sodium; 1 g carbohydrate; 0 g fiber; 3 g protein

Hot Cranberry Punch

Sip this hot punch and you'll discover a tea, orange juice, and cranberry blend that's oh-so-comforting.

MAKES 18 (4-ounce) servings **START TO FINISH** 25 minutes

- 4 cups water
- 2 cups cranberries
- 6 inches stick cinnamon
- 2 whole cloves
-    Peel from half an orange*
- 4 cups brewed tea
- ¾ cup sugar
- 1 6-ounce can frozen orange juice concentrate or ½ of a 6-ounce can frozen orange juice concentrate (⅓ cup) plus ½ of a 6-ounce can frozen lemonade concentrate (⅓ cup)
-    Orange slices
-    Stick cinnamon

① In a large saucepan or Dutch oven combine the water, cranberries, the 6 inches stick cinnamon, the cloves, and orange peel. Bring to boiling; reduce heat. Simmer, uncovered, for 5 minutes (cranberries will pop). Strain; discard solids. Return strained mixture to saucepan.

② Stir brewed tea, sugar, and orange juice concentrate into strained mixture. Cook and stir until sugar dissolves and mixture is heated through.

③ Serve in heatproof cups. Garnish with orange slices and additional cinnamon sticks.

***Tip:** Use a vegetable peeler to remove only the orange portion of the peel, leaving the white membrane on the fruit.

PER SERVING 56 calories; 0 g total fat; 0 mg cholesterol; 4 mg sodium; 14 g carbohydrate; 1 g fiber; 0 g protein

Champagne Punch

Toast the health of friends at the holidays, or any other time, with this refreshing citrus and champagne punch.

MAKES 10 (6-ounce) servings **START TO FINISH** 10 minutes

1 6-ounce can frozen orange juice concentrate, thawed
⅓ cup frozen lemonade concentrate, thawed
½ of a 750-ml bottle sweet white wine (such as Riesling), chilled
1 cup cold water
1 750-ml bottle champagne, chilled
   Ice cubes*

① In a punch bowl combine orange juice concentrate and lemonade concentrate. Add wine and the water; stir to combine.

② Add champagne, but do not stir. Serve immediately over ice cubes.

*Tip: If desired, make citrus ice cubes by putting small, thin slices of lemon, lime, and/or orange in an ice cube tray. Fill with water and freeze.

PER SERVING 132 calories; 0 g total fat; 0 mg cholesterol; 3 mg sodium; 15 g carbohydrate; 0 g fiber; 1 g protein

Bacon and Gorgonzola Cornbread Sliders with Chipotle Mayo

Love of cornbread runs in her family, admits Lori Stephens of Hendersonville, Tennessee. She says her family enjoys entering—and winning—the National Cornbread Festival Cook-Off, a recipe contest held in conjunction with the National Cornbread Festival in South Pittsburg, Tennessee. In 2010 Lori snagged the grand prize of $5,000 and a 30-inch FiveStar stainless-steel gas range with her Bacon and Gorgonzola Cornbread Sliders with Chipotle Mayo recipe. Lori earned first place in 2008, her grandmother captured first place in 2001, and Lori's mother and brother are former Cook-Off finalists. Now that's a family tradition!

MAKES 12 sliders **PREP** 50 minutes **BAKE** 12 minutes **COOK** 10 minutes **OVEN** 400°F

Nonstick cooking spray

2   6.5-ounce packages Martha White yellow cornbread mix or two 8.5-ounce packages yellow cornbread mix

½   cup Martha White all-purpose flour

1½ cups milk

¼   cup sour cream

1   egg, lightly beaten

¾   cup crumbled Gorgonzola cheese

8   slices bacon, crisp-cooked and crumbled

3   tablespoons snipped fresh chives

2   tablespoons butter

1   medium yellow onion, sliced and separated into rings

1½ pounds ground beef

1   egg

½   cup seasoned fine dry bread crumbs

2   cloves garlic, minced

1   teaspoon salt

½   teaspoon black pepper

12 0.5-ounce slices cheddar cheese

Chipotle Mayo

① Preheat oven to 400°F. Coat twelve 2½-inch cast-iron straight-sided muffin cups or regular muffin cups with cooking spray; set aside. In a medium bowl stir together cornbread mix and flour. Add milk, sour cream, and 1 egg, stirring until well mixed. Stir in Gorgonzola cheese, bacon, and chives. Spoon batter into prepared muffin cups, filling each about three-fourths full. Bake about 12 minutes or until golden brown and a wooden toothpick inserted near centers comes out clean. (Any remaining batter can be made into additional muffins.)

② In a 12-inch cast-iron or regular skillet melt butter on medium-low heat. Add onion. Cook and stir for 8 to 10 minutes or until onion is tender. Remove onion from skillet and set aside.

③ In a large bowl combine ground beef, 1 egg, bread crumbs, garlic, salt, and pepper; use your clean hands to mix well. Divide meat mixture into 12 portions. Pat each portion into a patty about ½ inch thick. In the same skillet cook patties, half at a time, on medium to medium-high heat for 10 to 12 minutes or until done (160°F), turning once. Top burgers with cheddar cheese.

④ Slice cornbread muffins in half horizontally. Spread Chipotle Mayo on cut sides of muffins. Place burgers on bottom muffin halves. Top with onion. Place muffin tops on burgers. Serve immediately.

Chipotle Mayo: In a small bowl combine ½ cup mayonnaise; 1 canned chipotle chile in adobo sauce, finely chopped;* and 1 teaspoon adobo sauce.

*Tip: Because chiles contain volatile oils that can burn your skin and eyes, avoid direct contact with them as much as possible. When working with chiles, wear plastic or rubber gloves. If your bare hands do touch the chiles, wash your hands and nails well with soap and warm water.

PER SLIDER 550 calories; 36 g total fat (14 g sat. fat); 114 mg cholesterol; 1,094 mg sodium; 33 g carbohydrate; 3 g fiber; 22 g protein

Bite-Size Chicken Empanadas

Show off these puff pastry bites as part of an appetizer buffet at your next cocktail party.

MAKES 48 empanadas **PREP** 35 minutes **MARINATE** 30 minutes **BROIL** 12 minutes **BAKE** 12 minutes **OVEN** 400°F

---

2 skinless, boneless chicken breast halves (8 to 12 ounces total)

2 tablespoons bottled French or Italian salad dressing

½ cup cooked rice

¼ cup shredded cheddar cheese (1 ounce)

¼ cup bottled salsa

¼ cup finely chopped red sweet pepper

2 tablespoons finely chopped green sweet pepper

2 tablespoons chopped ripe olives

2 tablespoons finely chopped onion

2 tablespoons sour cream

1 tablespoon finely chopped jalapeño*

1½ 17.25-ounce packages frozen puff pastry, thawed (3 sheets total)

1 egg, beaten

1 tablespoon water

① Place chicken in a shallow dish. Pour salad dressing over chicken. Cover and marinate chicken in refrigerator for 30 minutes.

② Meanwhile, preheat broiler. Drain chicken, discarding marinade. Place chicken on unheated rack of broiler pan. Broil 4 to 5 inches from heat for 12 to 15 minutes or until chicken is tender and no longer pink (170°F), turning once halfway through broiling. Cool slightly.

③ For filling, chop or shred chicken. In a large bowl combine chicken, rice, cheese, salsa, sweet peppers, olives, onion, sour cream, and jalapeño.

④ Preheat oven to 400°F. Lightly grease baking sheets; set aside. Place 1 sheet of the puff pastry on a lightly floured surface. (Keep remaining sheets covered until needed.) Roll puff pastry sheet to a 13-inch square. Using a 3-inch round cutter, cut pastry into 16 rounds. For each empanada, place a generous teaspoon of the chicken mixture slightly off center on each round. Brush edges of the pastry circles with cold water. Fold circles over the filling to make half-moon shapes. Pinch edges with fingers or a fork to seal tightly. Prick with a fork. Place on prepared baking sheet. In a small bowl combine egg and the 1 tablespoon water; brush over the empanadas. Repeat with the remaining puff pastry and the remaining filling.

⑤ Bake for 12 to 15 minutes or until golden brown. Serve warm.

*Tip: Because chiles contain volatile oils that can burn your skin and eyes, avoid direct contact with them as much as possible. When working with chiles, wear plastic or rubber gloves. If your bare hands do touch the chiles, wash your hands and nails well with soap and warm water.

PER EMPANADA 101 calories; 7 g total fat (2 g sat. fat); 8 mg cholesterol; 63 mg sodium; 8 g carbohydrate; 0 g fiber; 3 g protein

Grilling Directions: For charcoal grill, grill chicken on the rack of an uncovered grill directly over medium coals for 12 to 15 minutes or until chicken is tender and no longer pink (170°F), turning once halfway through grilling. (For a gas grill, preheat grill. Reduce heat to medium. Place chicken on grill rack over heat. Cover and grill as above.)

Ladder Loaf with Roasted Pepper Filling

This Italian-style ladder loaf, which is usually made with yeast dough, takes on an air of sophistication when you make it with puff pastry instead.

MAKES 24 servings **PREP** 55 minutes **STAND** 20 minutes **BAKE** 25 minutes **OVEN** 425°F

- 2 medium red, yellow, or orange sweet peppers
- 1½ cups firmly packed fresh spinach
- ½ cup firmly packed fresh basil
- ½ cup grated Parmesan cheese
- 1 clove garlic, quartered
- 1 egg, beaten
- 1 17.25-ounce package frozen puff pastry (2 sheets), thawed
- 2 tablespoons fine dry bread crumbs
- ¼ cup pine nuts or slivered almonds, toasted

① Preheat oven to 425°F. Line a baking sheet with foil. Set aside. Cut peppers into quarters and remove stems, membranes, and seeds. Place peppers, cut sides down, on prepared baking sheet. Bake for 20 to 25 minutes or until skins are bubbly and browned. Place the peppers in a bowl; cover tightly. Let stand for 20 to 30 minutes or until cool enough to handle. Using a paring knife, gently pull off the skins. Cut the pepper pieces into strips.

② Meanwhile, in a blender or food processor combine spinach, basil, Parmesan cheese, and garlic. Cover and blend or process with several on/off turns until well mixed. (Stop machine occasionally to scrape down sides.) Add 1 tablespoon of the beaten egg; blend or process until nearly smooth.

③ Line a baking sheet with parchment paper or plain brown paper. Unfold the pastry sheets. Carefully transfer 1 pastry sheet to the prepared baking sheet. (Keep the remaining pastry sheet covered until needed.) Brush pastry sheet with some of the remaining beaten egg. Sprinkle half of the bread crumbs in a 3-inch-wide strip down center of pastry. Spread half of the spinach-basil mixture on top of bread crumbs to within 1 inch of the ends. Sprinkle with half of the nuts. Arrange half of the pepper strips evenly over filling.

④ On both sides of filling, make 3-inch-long cuts from the edges toward the center at 1-inch intervals. Starting at one end, alternately fold opposite strips of dough at an angle across the filling. For second loaf, repeat with the remaining pastry sheet, bread crumbs, spinach-basil mixture, nuts, and pepper strips. Brush pastry with the remaining beaten egg.

⑤ Bake about 25 minutes or until golden brown. Serve warm or cooled. Cut each loaf crosswise into 6 slices; cut each lengthwise to make 12 pieces.

PER SERVING 71 calories; 5 g total fat (2 g sat. fat); 19 mg cholesterol; 107 mg sodium; 5 g carbohydrate; 1 g fiber; 3 g protein

Brie-Pecan Quesadillas

Chilling the Brie in the freezer for 30 minutes makes it much easier to chop the cheese for this super-easy appetizer.

MAKES 4 servings **START TO FINISH** 15 minutes

━━━━━━━◆━━━━━━━

3   ounces Brie cheese, chopped (about ¼ cup)
2   8- to 9-inch flour tortillas
2   tablespoons toasted chopped pecans or walnuts
2   tablespoons snipped fresh Italian (flat-leaf) parsley or regular parsley
¼   cup sour cream
    Fresh Italian (flat-leaf) parsley sprigs (optional)

① Sprinkle cheese over half of each tortilla. Top with nuts and the snipped parsley. Fold each tortilla in half, pressing gently.

② In a lightly greased 10-inch skillet or griddle cook folded tortillas on medium heat for 2 to 3 minutes or until lightly browned, turning once.

③ Cut quesadillas into wedges. Serve with sour cream and, if desired, garnish with parsley sprigs.

PER SERVING 192 calories; 12 g total fat (5 g sat. fat); 28 mg cholesterol; 269 mg sodium; 14 g carbohydrate; 0 g fiber; 7 g protein

Ham and Gouda Quesadillas: Prepare as directed, except substitute 1 cup shredded Gouda or smoked mozzarella cheese (4 ounces) for the Brie cheese and ½ cup chopped smoked ham for the pecans or walnuts.

PER SERVING 225 calories; 13 g total fat (7 g sat. fat); 48 mg cholesterol; 587 mg sodium; 14 g carbohydrate; 0 g fiber; 12 g protein.

Bourbon-Molasses-Glazed Chicken Wings

Asian chili sauce boosts the heat in the flavorful glaze on these wings.

MAKES 12 servings **PREP** 30 minutes
MARINATE 1 to 4 hours **BAKE** 50 minutes **OVEN** 375°F

━━━━━━━◆━━━━━━━

12   chicken wings (about 2 pounds total)
½   cup Dijon mustard
½   cup pure maple syrup
3   tablespoons cider vinegar
3   tablespoons molasses
2   tablespoons Asian chili sauce
2   tablespoons bourbon
2   teaspoons soy sauce
    Nonstick cooking spray
    Freshly ground black pepper

① Cut off and discard tips of chicken wings. Cut wings at joints to form 24 pieces. Place chicken wing pieces in a resealable plastic bag set in a shallow dish.

② For marinade, stir together mustard, maple syrup, vinegar, molasses, chili sauce, bourbon, and soy sauce. Pour over chicken wings. Seal bag; turn to coat chicken wings. Marinate in the refrigerator for 1 to 4 hours.

③ Preheat oven to 375°F. Line a shallow roasting pan with foil; lightly coat foil with cooking spray. Drain chicken wings, reserving marinade. Arrange wings in a single layer in prepared pan; sprinkle with pepper.

④ Bake for 30 minutes, spooning reserved marinade over wings twice. Turn wings over; spoon additional marinade over wings. Bake about 20 minutes more or until tender and no longer pink, spooning marinade over wings after 10 minutes. Discard any remaining marinade.

PER SERVING 148 calories; 6 g total fat (2 g sat. fat); 31 mg cholesterol; 338 mg sodium; 13 g carbohydrate; 0 g fiber; 8 g protein

Bourbon-Molasses-Glazed
Chicken Wings

Tomato Quiche Tartlets

Mini phyllo shells, each about 1¼ inches in diameter, are just right for two bites of these tiny cheese quiches.

MAKES 30 tartlets (15 servings) **PREP** 25 minutes
BAKE 10 minutes **OVEN** 325°F

———————◆———————

2	2.1-ounce packages baked miniature phyllo dough shells (15 per package; 30 total)
½	cup finely snipped dried tomatoes (not oil pack)
2	eggs, beaten
3	tablespoons half-and-half, light cream, or milk
1½	teaspoons snipped fresh basil or ½ teaspoon dried basil, crushed
	Dash salt
	Dash black pepper
3	ounces Emmentaler cheese or Swiss cheese, finely shredded (¾ cup)

① Preheat oven to 325°F. Place phyllo dough shells on an ungreased baking sheet; set aside.

② For filling, cover snipped dried tomatoes with boiling water; let stand for 2 minutes. Drain well; set aside. In a medium bowl stir together eggs, half-and-half, basil, salt, and pepper. Stir in drained tomatoes and cheese.

③ Spoon 2 teaspoons of the filling into each shell. Bake for 10 to 15 minutes or just until slightly puffed and a small knife inserted into the centers of the tartlets comes out clean. Serve warm or cooled.

PER SERVING 85 calories; 5 g total fat (1 g sat. fat); 35 mg cholesterol; 82 mg sodium; 6 g carbohydrate; 0 g fiber; 4 g protein

Mexican Meatballs

Spice up the sauce to suit your taste. Gradually add the chile puree, tasting after each addition and stopping when you reach the desired heat level.

MAKES 84 meatballs **PREP** 45 minutes **COOK** 30 minutes

———————◆———————

6	cloves garlic
1½	teaspoons salt
½	cup masa harina (corn tortilla flour)
¼	cup warm water
1	pound lean ground pork
1	pound lean ground beef
1	egg
½	teaspoon freshly ground black pepper
2	28-ounce cans tomatoes, drained
1	cup water
3	canned chipotle chiles in adobo sauce, drained
¼	cup vegetable oil
½	cup chopped onion (1 medium)
2	tablespoons instant chicken bouillon granules
1	teaspoon ground cumin
	Snipped fresh parsley or cilantro (optional)

① In a small bowl combine 4 of the garlic cloves and ½ teaspoon of the salt; use a fork to mash until a paste forms. In a large bowl combine masa harina and the ¼ cup warm water. Add pork, beef, egg, the garlic paste, the remaining 1 teaspoon salt, and the black pepper; mix well. Shape mixture into 1-inch balls.

② For sauce, in a blender combine tomatoes and the remaining 2 garlic cloves. Cover and blend until smooth; press mixture through a sieve into a small bowl. In the blender combine the 1 cup water and the chiles. Cover and blend until smooth; press mixture through a sieve into another small bowl.

③ In a large Dutch oven heat oil on medium heat. Add onion; cook and stir for 2 minutes. Add tomato mixture. Cook, covered, for 5 minutes. Stir in bouillon granules and cumin; cook for 2 minutes more. Gradually add the chile puree, tasting for spiciness after each addition.

④ Add meatballs to sauce in Dutch oven. Bring to boiling. Cook, covered, for 3 minutes. Reduce heat. Simmer, covered, for 30 minutes, turning meatballs occasionally. If desired, garnish with parsley.

PER MEATBALL 38 calories; 2 g total fat (1 g sat. fat); 10 mg cholesterol; 145 mg sodium; 2 g carbohydrate; 0 g fiber; 2 g protein

Mexican Meatballs

Vidalia Sweetest Onion-Licious Pie

Known around the world for its sweet onions, Vidalia, Georgia, has hosted a five-day Vidalia Onion Festival each spring since 1978. The festival showcases an abundance of fun activities, including a culinary contest. Sabrina Toole of Vidalia, Georgia, won first place in the 2009 Vidalia Onion Cook-Off with her Vidalia Sweetest Onion-Licious Pie. Sabrina cuts it into wedges and serves it hot as a tempting appetizer or tasty side dish. It's the epitome of all things Southern!

MAKES 10 servings **PREP** 20 minutes **COOK** 12 minutes **BAKE** 30 minutes
STAND 15 minutes **OVEN** 350°F

54	**rich round crackers, crumbled (2¼ cups crumbled)**
6	**tablespoons butter, softened**
2	**cups thinly sliced sweet Vidalia onions**
2	**cloves garlic, minced**
2	**eggs**
¾	**cup whipping cream**
½	**teaspoon salt**
¾	**cup shredded Swiss cheese (3 ounces)**

① Preheat oven to 350°F. For crust, in a medium bowl combine crackers and 4 tablespoons of the butter, stirring until well mixed. Press cracker mixture into the bottom and up the sides of a 9-inch pie plate. Bake about 5 minutes or until light golden brown. Cool on a wire rack.

② In a large skillet melt the remaining 2 tablespoons butter on medium heat. Add onions and garlic; cook and stir about 12 minutes or until tender.

③ Spread cooked onion mixture in the crust. In a medium bowl beat together eggs, cream, and salt. Pour mixture over onions. Sprinkle with cheese.

④ Bake for 30 to 35 minutes or until a knife inserted into the center comes out clean. Let stand for 15 minutes before serving. To serve, cut into wedges.

PER SERVING 270 calories; 21 g total fat (11 g sat. fat); 93 mg cholesterol; 350 mg sodium; 15 g carbohydrate; 1 g fiber; 5 g protein

Cheese-Stuffed Jalapeños

Cool the heat from these stuffed jalapeños by dipping them in salsa. (Pictured on page 6.)

MAKES 20 stuffed jalapeños **START TO FINISH** 1 hour
OVEN 300°F

- 20 fresh jalapeños*
- 1 cup shredded Monterey Jack cheese (4 ounces)
- ½ of an 8-ounce tub cream cheese with chive and onion
- ¼ teaspoon ground cumin
- 1½ cups all-purpose flour
- ½ cup cornmeal
- 1 teaspoon salt
- ½ teaspoon baking powder
- 1 12-ounce can beer or 1½ cups milk
  Cooking oil or shortening for deep-fat frying
  Bottled salsa (optional)

① Make a T-shape cut in the side of each jalapeño; remove seeds and membranes.*

② For filling, in a small bowl stir together shredded cheese, cream cheese, and cumin. Pack about 2 teaspoons of the filling into the cut in each jalapeño.

③ For batter, in a medium bowl combine flour, cornmeal, salt, and baking powder. Add beer or milk. Beat until smooth.

④ Preheat oven to 300°F. In a heavy saucepan or deep-fat fryer heat 2 inches cooking oil or melted shortening to 375°F. Dip stuffed peppers into batter. Fry jalapeños, several at a time, in hot fat about 4 minutes or until golden brown, turning once. Drain on paper towels. Transfer to a baking sheet; keep warm in oven while frying the remaining jalapeños. If desired, serve with salsa.

*Tip: Because chiles contain volatile oils that can burn your skin and eyes, avoid direct contact with them as much as possible. When working with chiles, wear plastic or rubber gloves. If your bare hands do touch the chiles, wash your hands and nails well with soap and warm water.

PER STUFFED JALAPEÑO 140 calories; 8 g total fat (3 g sat. fat); 11 mg cholesterol; 179 mg sodium; 12 g carbohydrate; 1 g fiber; 3 g protein

Tequila-Marinated Shrimp

To keep these lime-and-cilantro shrimp well chilled during a party, place them in a bowl nestled inside a larger bowl of ice.

MAKES 10 to 12 servings **PREP** 30 minutes
CHILL 2 to 24 hours

- 2 pounds fresh or frozen medium shrimp
- ¼ cup olive oil
- 3 tablespoons finely chopped onion
- 5 cloves garlic, minced
- ¼ cup tequila
- ¼ cup lime juice
- 2 tablespoons snipped fresh cilantro
- ⅛ teaspoon salt

① Thaw shrimp, if frozen. Peel and devein shrimp, leaving tails intact if desired. Rinse shrimp; pat dry with paper towels. Set aside.

② In a large skillet heat oil on medium heat. Add onion and garlic; cook about 3 minutes or until tender. Add shrimp and tequila; bring to boiling. Boil gently, uncovered, for 3 to 5 minutes or until shrimp turn opaque, stirring occasionally.

③ Transfer shrimp mixture to a large bowl. Add lime juice, cilantro, and salt; toss to mix. Cover and refrigerate for 2 to 24 hours, stirring occasionally. Drain before serving.

PER SERVING 119 calories; 6 g total fat (1 g sat. fat); 105 mg cholesterol; 147 mg sodium; 1 g carbohydrate; 0 g fiber; 11 g protein

Toasted Almonds with Rosemary and Cayenne

Sweet, hot, and crunchy—no wonder these herb-coated almonds disappear in a flash. Set out a bowl or two, especially when you're serving cocktails.

MAKES 16 servings **START TO FINISH** 20 minutes **OVEN** 350°F

8	ounces unblanched almonds or pecan halves (about 2 cups)
1½	teaspoons butter or margarine
1	tablespoon finely snipped fresh rosemary
1½	teaspoons packed brown sugar
¼ to ½	teaspoon salt
¼	teaspoon cayenne pepper

① Preheat oven to 350°F. Spread nuts in a single layer on a baking sheet. Bake about 10 minutes or until nuts are lightly toasted and fragrant.

② Meanwhile, in a medium saucepan melt butter over medium heat until sizzling. Remove from heat. Stir in rosemary, brown sugar, salt, and cayenne pepper. Add nuts to butter mixture and toss to coat. Cool slightly before serving.

Make-Ahead Directions: Prepare as directed. Transfer cooled nuts to an airtight container. Store in the refrigerator for up to 1 month or in the freezer for up to 3 months.

PER SERVING 80 calories; 7 g total fat (1 g sat. fat); 2 mg cholesterol; 37 mg sodium; 3 g carbohydrate; 1 g fiber; 4 g protein

Chapter 2

BRING ON
BREAKFAST

The secret to a great day: Start it with one of these fantastic dishes.

Orange Sticky Rolls

EGG AND CHEESE DISHES

Eggs in Purgatory with
Artichoke Hearts,
Potatoes, and Capers, 35

French Onion Omelet, 33

Overnight Egg and
Sausage Strata, 32

Popover Egg Nests, 30

Salmon and Eggs
Benedict with Easy
Hollandaise, 31

Zucchini and Feta Cheese
Soufflés, 33

PANCAKES, FRENCH TOAST, AND WAFFLES

Double Chocolate-
Strawberry Pancakes, 39

No-Fry French Toast, 37

Pecan-Molasses
Waffles, 41

Sunrise Whole Wheat
Griddle Cakes, 36

FRUIT DISHES

Gingered Melon, 48

Minted Fruit Compote, 48

BREAKFAST BREADS

Blueberry Breakfast
Scones, 45

Breakfast Popovers, 47

Cream Cheese and
Raspberry Coffee
Cake, 44

Cream Cheese-Pumpkin
Muffins, 47

Doughnut Muffins, 46

Dried Cherry Scones, 45

Orange Sticky Rolls, 40

Pecan-Praline
Cinnamon Rolls, 43

Popover Egg Nests

These poached eggs tucked into popovers and accented with a lime hollandaise sauce add a flavorful touch to any brunch.

MAKES 6 servings **PREP** 45 minutes **BAKE** 40 minutes **OVEN** 400°F

½ cup butter
    Shortening or nonstick cooking spray
2 eggs
1 cup milk
1 tablespoon vegetable oil
1 cup all-purpose flour
¼ teaspoon salt
6 eggs
3 egg yolks, lightly beaten
1 tablespoon water
1 tablespoon lime juice
⅛ teaspoon salt
6 thin slices prosciutto, Canadian bacon, or cooked ham (about 4 ounces)
    Finely shredded lime peel (optional)
    Lime wedges (optional)

① Cut butter into thirds and bring to room temperature. For popovers, preheat oven to 400°F. Using ½ teaspoon shortening for each cup, grease the bottoms and sides of six 6-ounce custard cups or popover pan cups. Or coat cups with cooking spray. Place custard cups in a 15 x 10 x 1-inch baking pan. Set aside.

② In a medium bowl whisk together the 2 eggs, milk, and oil until combined. Add flour and the ¼ teaspoon salt; beat until smooth. Spoon batter into the prepared cups, filling each about half full. Bake about 40 minutes or until golden brown and very firm.

③ Meanwhile, for poached eggs, lightly grease a large skillet. Half fill the skillet with water. Bring water to boiling; reduce heat to simmering (bubbles should begin to break the surface of the water).

④ Break 1 of the 6 eggs into a cup and slip egg into the simmering water, holding the lip of the cup as close to the water as possible. Repeat with the remaining 5 eggs, allowing each egg an equal amount of space in the water.

⑤ Simmer eggs, uncovered, for 3 to 5 minutes or until whites are completely set and yolks begin to thicken but are not hard. Carefully remove eggs with a slotted spoon and place them in a large shallow pan of hot water to keep them warm while preparing the sauce.

⑥ For sauce, in the top of a double boiler combine egg yolks, the 1 tablespoon water, lime juice, and the ⅛ teaspoon salt. Add a piece of the butter. Place over boiling water (upper pan should not touch water). Cook, stirring rapidly with a whisk, until butter is melted and sauce begins to thicken. Add the remaining butter, 1 piece at a time, stirring constantly until melted. Continue to cook and stir about 2 minutes more or until sauce is thickened. Immediately remove from heat. If sauce is too thick or curdles, immediately whisk in 1 to 2 tablespoons hot water.

⑦ Immediately after removing popovers from oven, prick each popover with a fork to let steam escape. Turn off oven. For crisper popovers, return popovers to oven for 5 to 10 minutes or until desired crispness is reached. Remove popovers from cups.

⑧ For each serving, split a popover in half and place on a plate. Top with 1 slice of the prosciutto, a poached egg, and about 2 tablespoons of the sauce. If desired, garnish with lime peel and serve with lime wedges.

PER SERVING 452 calories; 35 g total fat (14 g sat. fat); 434 mg cholesterol; 730 mg sodium; 18 g carbohydrate; 0 g fiber; 18 g protein

Salmon and Eggs Benedict with Easy Hollandaise

Boost your reputation as a terrific cook with this spectacular breakfast entrée that showcases lox-style salmon and poached eggs on crispy English muffins topped off with a dill-sprinkled hollandaise sauce.

MAKES 4 servings **START TO FINISH** 25 minutes

4	**eggs**
⅓	**cup sour cream**
⅓	**cup mayonnaise**
1	**tablespoon drained capers (optional)**
2	**teaspoons lemon juice**
1	**teaspoon yellow mustard**
½	**teaspoon dried dill**
	Milk (optional)
2	**English muffins, split**
¼	**cup tub-style cream cheese spread with chive and onion, softened**
4	**ounces thinly sliced smoked salmon (lox-style)**
	Dried dill (optional)

① Preheat broiler. For poached eggs, lightly grease a large skillet. Half fill the skillet with water. Bring water to boiling; reduce heat to simmering (bubbles should begin to break the surface of the water). Break 1 of the eggs into a cup and slip egg into the simmering water, holding the lip of the cup as close to the water as possible. Repeat with the remaining 3 eggs, allowing each egg an equal amount of space in the water.

② Simmer eggs, uncovered, for 3 to 5 minutes or until whites are completely set and yolks begin to thicken but are not hard. Carefully remove eggs with a slotted spoon and place in a large shallow pan of hot water to keep them warm while preparing the sauce.

③ For sauce, in a small saucepan combine sour cream, mayonnaise, capers (if desired), lemon juice, mustard, and the ½ teaspoon dill. Cook and stir on medium-low heat until warm. If desired, stir in a little milk to thin sauce.

④ Place muffin halves, cut sides up, on a baking sheet. Broil 3 to 4 inches from the heat about 2 minutes or until brown. Spread 1 tablespoon of the cream cheese spread on each muffin half. Top with salmon. Broil about 1 minute more or until salmon is warm.

⑤ To serve, top muffin halves with poached eggs; spoon sauce over eggs. If desired, sprinkle with additional dill.

Make-Ahead Directions: Prepare the eggs and toast English muffins as directed. Place muffin halves in a greased 8 x 8 x 2-inch baking pan. Top with cream cheese spread, salmon, and poached eggs. Cover and chill for 2 to 24 hours. To serve, preheat oven to 350°F. Prepare sauce; spoon warm sauce over eggs. Bake, covered, about 30 minutes or until heated through.

PER SERVING 391 calories; 30 g total fat (10 g sat. fat); 248 mg cholesterol; 1161 mg sodium; 15 g carbohydrate; 1 g fiber; 15 g protein

Overnight Egg and Sausage Strata

This strata is perfect for a relaxed family morning meal or a company-special brunch. Use crusty bread for a firm baked custard or soft bread for a lighter soufflélike texture.

MAKES 8 servings **PREP** 40 minutes **CHILL** overnight **STAND** 1 hour **BAKE** 55 minutes **OVEN** 350°F

8	ounces sweet or hot bulk Italian sausage
2	teaspoons olive oil
2	cups sweet red pepper strips (2 medium)
2	medium onions, thinly sliced
¼	teaspoon salt
1	1-pound loaf French or Italian bread, cut into ½-inch slices and quartered
1	cup shredded fontina cheese (4 ounces)
4	eggs
5	cups light (1%) milk
¾	teaspoon salt
⅛	teaspoon black pepper

① In a large nonstick skillet cook sausage on medium-high heat until brown, using a wooden spoon to break up meat as it cooks. Drain sausage in a colander.

② In the same skillet heat oil on medium heat. Add sweet peppers, onions, and the ¼ teaspoon salt. Cook about 15 minutes or until vegetables are light brown, stirring occasionally.

③ Place half of the bread in an ungreased 3-quart rectangular baking dish. Top with half of the sausage, half of the sweet pepper mixture, and ½ cup of the cheese. Repeat layers.

④ In a large bowl combine eggs, milk, the ¾ teaspoon salt, and black pepper. Pour egg mixture evenly over layers in baking dish. Using the back of a spoon, gently press down on layers. Cover with plastic wrap and chill overnight.

⑤ Let strata stand at room temperature for 1 hour before baking. Preheat oven to 350°F. Remove plastic wrap from strata; cover with foil. Bake for 30 minutes. Bake, uncovered, for 25 to 30 minutes more or until light brown and set in center.

PER SERVING 436 calories; 20 g total fat (8 g sat. fat); 151 mg cholesterol; 1,046 mg sodium; 41 g carbohydrate; 3 g fiber; 21 g protein

Zucchini and Feta Cheese Soufflés

Serve these mini Mediterranean soufflés with a fresh fruit salad for brunch or as a side dish with fish.

MAKES 6 servings **PREP** 20 minutes
STAND 30 minutes **BAKE** 20 minutes **OVEN** 375°F

2 cups shredded zucchini
1 teaspoon salt
3 tablespoons butter
¼ cup all-purpose flour
1 teaspoon dry mustard
¼ cup milk
½ cup crumbled feta cheese (2 ounces)
1 tablespoon grated Parmesan cheese
4 egg yolks
4 egg whites

① Place zucchini in a colander; sprinkle with salt and toss lightly. Let stand for 30 minutes. Rinse and drain. Squeeze out excess liquid; set aside. Preheat oven to 375°F. Grease six 6-ounce soufflé dishes or custard cups; set aside.

② In a medium saucepan heat butter on medium heat until melted. Stir in flour and dry mustard. Add milk all at once. Cook and stir until thickened and bubbly. Remove from heat. Stir in zucchini, feta cheese, and Parmesan cheese. In a medium bowl beat yolks with a fork until combined. Gradually stir in zucchini mixture.

③ In a large bowl beat egg whites with an electric mixer on medium to high until stiff peaks form (tips stand straight). Gently fold about 1 cup of the beaten egg whites into zucchini mixture. Gradually add zucchini mixture to the remaining beaten egg whites, folding gently to combine. Spoon into the prepared soufflé dishes.

④ Bake for 20 to 25 minutes or until a knife inserted near centers comes out clean. Serve immediately.

PER SERVING 174 calories; 12 g total fat (6 g sat. fat); 169 mg cholesterol; 276 mg sodium; 8 g carbohydrate; 1 g fiber; 8 g protein

French Onion Omelet

Here's one omelet you don't have to flip. It bakes in a skillet in the oven.

MAKES 6 servings **PREP** 25 minutes
BAKE 15 minutes **OVEN** 375°F

1 tablespoon olive oil
2 cups coarsely chopped red onions (2 large)
¼ cup chopped shallots (2 medium) (optional)
2 teaspoons sugar
¼ cup sliced green onions (2)
2 teaspoons Dijon mustard
½ teaspoon dried thyme, crushed
6 eggs
¼ cup water
¼ teaspoon salt
¼ teaspoon white pepper
1 cup shredded Swiss cheese (4 ounces)

① Preheat oven to 375°F. In a large oven-going skillet heat oil on medium heat. Add red onions, shallots (if desired), and sugar. Cook for 12 to 15 minutes or until onions are tender and golden brown, stirring occasionally. Remove ¼ cup of the cooked onion mixture and set aside. Stir green onions, mustard, and thyme into the remaining cooked onion mixture.

② In a medium bowl beat together eggs, the water, salt, and pepper. Stir in ¾ cup of the cheese. Pour over mixture in skillet. Bake about 15 minutes or until set. Top with the remaining ¼ cup cheese and the reserved ¼ cup cooked onion mixture. Cut into wedges.

PER SERVING 202 calories; 13 g total fat (5 g sat. fat); 230 mg cholesterol; 245 mg sodium; 9 g carbohydrate; 1 g fiber; 13 g protein

Eggs in Purgatory with Artichoke Hearts, Potatoes, and Capers

Salinas, California, food blogger Debby Farmer loves cooking mouthwatering meals for her son, Brian, and hubby, Craig, and is always looking for captivating recipes. When she spotted Eggs in Purgatory with Artichoke Hearts, Potatoes, and Capers while perusing her March 2010 issue of Bon Appetit, *Debby knew she just had to make it. Deciding to scale back on the serving size and bake it in her beloved cast-iron skillet (fewer dishes to wash), Debby adapted the magazine's recipe. It's no surprise this colorful and hearty vegetarian dish won Debby a prize from the Eggland's Best Eggs recipe contest.*

MAKES 6 servings **PREP** 40 minutes **BAKE** 12 minutes **OVEN** 375°F

2	tablespoons olive oil
1½	cups chopped onions (3 medium)
2	teaspoons snipped fresh thyme
½	teaspoon crushed red pepper
¼	teaspoon kosher salt
¼	teaspoon freshly ground black pepper
1	8- or 9-ounce package frozen artichoke hearts, thawed and drained
2	cloves garlic, minced
1	28-ounce or two 14.5-ounce cans fire-roasted diced tomatoes, undrained
8	ounces potatoes, peeled and cut into ½-inch pieces
2	tablespoons drained capers
	Kosher salt
	Freshly ground black pepper
6	eggs
⅓	cup freshly grated Parmesan cheese

① Preheat oven to 375°F. In a large oven-going* skillet heat oil on medium heat. Add onions, thyme, crushed red pepper, the ¼ teaspoon salt, and the ¼ teaspoon black pepper. Cook about 10 minutes or until onions are tender and golden brown, stirring occasionally.

② Add artichokes and garlic; cook and stir for 1 minute. Stir in tomatoes. Bring to boiling; reduce heat. Simmer, covered, for 15 minutes to allow flavors to blend.

③ Meanwhile, in a covered medium saucepan cook potatoes in a small amount of boiling salted water about 8 minutes or just until tender; drain. (The potatoes will continue to cook in the oven; avoid overcooking or they'll become mushy.)

④ Stir potatoes and capers into tomato mixture. Simmer, covered, for 5 minutes. Season to taste with additional salt and black pepper.

⑤ Using the back of a spoon, make 6 evenly spaced indentations in tomato mixture. Break 1 egg into each indentation. (Some of the eggs may run together slightly in spots.) Bake for 12 to 16 minutes or until eggs are desired doneness. Sprinkle with cheese.

*Tip: If you don't have a large oven-going skillet, use a large regular skillet, but transfer the tomato mixture to an ungreased 3-quart rectangular baking dish before adding the eggs.

PER SERVING 221 calories; 11 g total fat (3 g sat. fat); 215 mg cholesterol; 627 mg sodium; 21 g carbohydrate; 5 g fiber; 11 g protein

Sunrise Whole Wheat Griddle Cakes

Nuts, apricot nectar, and whole grain goodness—that's what goes into this sunrise pancake feast. Add some crispy bacon and you're in business for a hearty breakfast or brunch.

MAKES 6 to 8 servings (18 pancakes) **START TO FINISH** 30 minutes

1	12-ounce can apricot nectar
4	teaspoons cornstarch
2	tablespoons honey
1	tablespoon butter
¼	teaspoon finely shredded lemon peel
1	tablespoon lemon juice
1½	cups all-purpose flour
1½	cups whole wheat flour
1	tablespoon baking powder
1	tablespoon packed brown sugar
½	teaspoon salt
2	eggs, lightly beaten
2	cups milk
3	tablespoons vegetable oil
½	cup chopped pecans
	Butter (optional)

① For sauce, in a small saucepan stir together apricot nectar and cornstarch. Cook and stir on medium heat until thickened and bubbly. Cook and stir for 2 minutes more. Stir in honey, the 1 tablespoon butter, lemon peel, and lemon juice. Cook and stir until butter is melted. Remove from heat; cover and keep warm.

② In a large bowl stir together all-purpose flour, whole wheat flour, baking powder, brown sugar, and salt.

③ In a medium bowl combine eggs, milk, and oil. Add egg mixture all at once to flour mixture. Stir just until moistened (batter should be slightly lumpy). Stir in pecans.

④ For each pancake, pour about ¼ cup of the batter onto a hot, lightly greased griddle or heavy skillet. If necessary, spread batter into a 4-inch circle. Cook on medium heat for 2 to 4 minutes or until pancakes are golden brown, turning when surfaces are bubbly and edges are slightly dry. Serve warm pancakes with sauce and, if desired, additional butter.

PER SERVING 477 calories; 19 g total fat (5 g sat. fat); 82 mg cholesterol; 482 mg sodium; 66 g carbohydrate; 6 g fiber; 13 g protein

No-Fry French Toast

Once you try this French toast, you'll never make it the old-fashioned way again. On a griddle or in a skillet, French toast must be made in batches, but with this baked recipe you can make eight slices at once.

MAKES 4 servings **PREP** 15 minutes **BAKE** 11 minutes **OVEN** 450°F

Nonstick cooking spray
1   egg, lightly beaten
1   egg white, lightly beaten
¾   cup fat-free milk
1   teaspoon vanilla
⅛   teaspoon ground cinnamon
8   1-inch-thick slices firm-texture French bread
¼   teaspoon finely shredded orange peel
½   cup orange juice
1   tablespoon honey
1   teaspoon cornstarch
⅛   teaspoon ground cinnamon
1   tablespoon powdered sugar (optional)

① Preheat oven to 450°F. Coat a large baking sheet with cooking spray; set aside. In a shallow bowl combine egg, egg white, milk, vanilla, and ⅛ teaspoon cinnamon. Dip bread into egg mixture, coating both sides (let bread soak in egg mixture about 30 seconds per side). Place on the prepared baking sheet.

② Bake about 6 minutes or until bread is light brown. Turn bread over and bake for 5 to 8 minutes more or until golden brown.

③ Meanwhile, for orange syrup, in a small saucepan stir together orange peel, orange juice, honey, cornstarch, and ⅛ teaspoon cinnamon. Cook and stir on medium heat until thickened and bubbly. Cook and stir for 2 minutes more.

④ If desired, sprinkle toast lightly with powdered sugar. Serve with warm orange syrup.

Tip: If you are using soft-texture bread, reduce the soaking time.

PER SERVING 212 calories; 3 g total fat (1 g sat. fat); 54 mg cholesterol; 358 mg sodium; 37 g carbohydrate; 2 g fiber; 9 g protein

Double Chocolate-Strawberry Pancakes

"Measure precisely, don't overmix the pancake batter (it should be slightly lumpy), and definitely use strawberry extract—it really does taste authentic and makes the baked goods burst with strawberry flavor," says Joni Hilton of Rocklin, California. Her recipe for Double Chocolate-Strawberry Pancakes was the $1,000 first place winner of the 2010 Bisquick® Recipe Contest. "This is a true flavor blast of chocolate and strawberry— double doses of each! Everyone loves chocolate-dipped strawberries," Joni says, "so I thought a pancake combining those yummy flavors would be a real hit." They were!

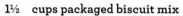

MAKES 14 pancakes **PREP** 20 minutes **COOK** 5 minutes per batch

1½ cups packaged biscuit mix
¼ cup unsweetened cocoa powder
2 eggs, lightly beaten
1 8-ounce carton sour cream
½ cup milk
2 teaspoons strawberry extract or vanilla
1 cup semisweet chocolate pieces
2 cups sliced fresh strawberries
   Strawberry-flavor pancake syrup
   Whipped cream or frozen whipped dessert topping, thawed

① In a large bowl stir together biscuit mix and cocoa powder. In a small bowl combine eggs, sour cream, milk, and strawberry extract. Add egg mixture all at once to flour mixture. Stir just until moistened (batter should be slightly lumpy). Gently stir in chocolate pieces.

② For each pancake, pour about ¼ cup of the batter onto a hot, lightly greased griddle or heavy skillet. Spread batter into a 3½- to 4-inch circle. Cook on medium heat about 3 minutes or until surfaces are puffed and edges are slightly dry. Turn and cook about 2 minutes more or until brown. (If pancakes brown too quickly, reduce heat to medium-low.)

③ Serve warm. Top pancakes with strawberries, syrup, and whipped cream.

Tip: This batter is somewhat thick. If you like, add a little more milk for thinner pancakes.

PER PANCAKE 248 calories; 13 g total fat (6 g sat. fat); 39 mg cholesterol; 204 mg sodium; 33 g carbohydrate; 2 g fiber; 3 g protein

Orange Sticky Rolls

Moist, with a kiss of citrus, these warm-from-the-oven sweet rolls will bring smiles to the faces of kids and grown-ups alike.

MAKES 24 rolls **PREP** 25 minutes **RISE** 1½ hours **BAKE** 18 minutes **OVEN** 375°F

3½ **to 4 cups all-purpose flour**
1 **package active dry yeast**
1¼ **cups milk**
2 **tablespoons sugar**
2 **tablespoons shortening**
1 **teaspoon salt**
1 **egg**
1 **cup sugar**
½ **cup butter, softened**
2 **tablespoons finely shredded orange peel**
   Powdered Sugar Icing (optional)

① In a large bowl combine 1½ cups of the flour and the yeast; set aside. In a medium saucepan heat and stir milk, the 2 tablespoons sugar, shortening, and salt just until warm (120°F to 130°F) and shortening almost melts.

② Add milk mixture to flour mixture; add egg. Beat with an electric mixer on low to medium for 30 seconds, scraping sides of bowl constantly. Beat on high for 3 minutes. Using a wooden spoon, stir in as much of the remaining flour as you can.

③ Turn dough out onto a lightly floured surface. Knead in enough of the remaining flour to make a moderately soft dough that is smooth and elastic (3 to 5 minutes total).

④ Shape dough into a ball. Place in a lightly greased bowl, turning once to grease surface. Cover and let rise in a warm place until double in size (about 1 hour).

⑤ Punch dough down. Turn out onto a lightly floured surface. Divide in half. Cover and let rest for 10 minutes. Lightly grease two 9 x 1½-inch round baking pans. For filling, in a small bowl combine the 1 cup sugar, butter, and orange peel.

⑥ Roll each portion of dough into a 12 x 8-inch rectangle. Spread each rectangle with filling, leaving about 1 inch unfilled along the long sides. Roll up each rectangle, starting from a filled long side; pinch dough to seal seams. Slice each roll into twelve 1-inch pieces. Place in the prepared baking pans. Cover and let rise in a warm place until nearly double in size (about 30 minutes).

⑦ Preheat oven to 375°F. Bake for 18 to 20 minutes or until golden brown. Cool in pans on wire racks for 2 minutes; remove from pans. If desired, drizzle with Powdered Sugar Icing.

Powdered Sugar Icing: In a small bowl stir together 2 cups powdered sugar, 1 tablespoon orange juice or milk, and ½ teaspoon vanilla. Stir in 1 to 2 tablespoons additional orange juice or milk, 1 teaspoon at a time, to make an icing of drizzling consistency.

PER ROLL 157 calories; 5 g total fat (3 g sat. fat); 20 mg cholesterol; 133 mg sodium; 24 g carbohydrate; 1 g fiber; 3 g protein

Pecan-Molasses Waffles

For a Texas-style weekend breakfast, bake these tender molasses-sweetened waffles with pecans added to the batter.

MAKES 9 waffles **START TO FINISH** 35 minutes

1½ **cups all-purpose flour**
1 **tablespoon baking powder**
½ **teaspoon baking soda**
½ **teaspoon salt**
2 **egg yolks**
¾ **cup milk**
¼ **cup molasses**
3 **tablespoons vegetable oil**
1 **teaspoon finely shredded orange peel**
¼ **cup finely chopped pecans**
2 **egg whites**
   Butter (optional)
   Pecan halves (optional)
   Maple syrup (optional)

① In a large bowl stir together flour, baking powder, baking soda, and salt. In a small bowl combine egg yolks, milk, molasses, oil, and orange peel. Add egg mixture all at once to flour mixture. Stir just until moistened (batter should be slightly lumpy). Stir in the chopped pecans.

② In another small bowl beat egg whites with an electric mixer on medium-high until soft peaks form (tips curl). Fold into batter.

③ Add batter to a preheated, lightly greased waffle baker according to the manufacturer's directions. Close lid quickly; do not open until done. Bake according to the manufacturer's directions. When done, use a fork to lift waffle off grid. Repeat with the remaining batter. Serve warm. If desired, serve with butter, the pecan halves, and maple syrup.

PER WAFFLE 200 calories; 10 g total fat (2 g sat. fat); 50 mg cholesterol; 335 mg sodium; 24 g carbohydrate; 1 g fiber; 4 g protein

Pecan-Praline Cinnamon Rolls

"Nothing whets the appetite like the tempting fragrance of homemade cinnamon rolls baking in the oven," confesses Nancy Johnson of Story City, Iowa. Always a huge hit with her family and friends, Nancy's Pecan-Praline Cinnamon Rolls earned her $3,000 and the coveted First Place overall title awarded by Iowa State Fair judges in the 2009 Tone's Cinnamon Roll Contest. "I love baking bread," Nancy says. "I've been baking since I was a 4-H member during grade school."

MAKES 24 rolls **PREP** 45 minutes **RISE** 2 hours **BAKE** 25 minutes **COOL** 5 minutes **OVEN** 350°F

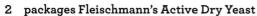

2   packages Fleischmann's Active Dry Yeast
½   cup warm water (100°F to 110°F)
1½   cups milk
¾   cup butter
7½   to 8 cups all-purpose flour
⅔   cup granulated sugar
2   eggs
2   teaspoons salt
½   cup granulated sugar
1½   tablespoons Tone's Ground Cinnamon
1½   cups packed brown sugar
6   tablespoons butter
⅓   cup Karo Light Corn Syrup
2   tablespoons water
⅛   teaspoon salt
1½   cups pecan halves, toasted*
¼   cup butter, softened

① In a large bowl dissolve yeast in the ½ cup warm water. In a small saucepan heat and stir milk and the ¾ cup butter just until warm (100°F to 110°F) and butter almost melts. Add to yeast mixture. Add 3 cups of the flour, the ⅔ cup granulated sugar, eggs, and the 2 teaspoons salt. Beat with an electric mixer on low to medium for 30 seconds, scraping sides of bowl constantly. Beat on high for 3 minutes. Using a wooden spoon, stir in as much of the remaining flour as you can.

② Turn dough out onto a lightly floured surface. Knead in enough of the remaining flour to make a moderately soft dough that is smooth and elastic (3 to 5 minutes total). (Or knead with a stand mixer using a dough hook.) Shape dough into a ball. Place in a lightly greased bowl, turning once to grease surface. Cover and let rise in a warm place until double in size (about 1 hour).

③ For filling, in a small bowl combine the ½ cup granulated sugar and cinnamon; set aside.

④ For topping, in a medium heavy saucepan combine brown sugar, the 6 tablespoons butter, corn syrup, the 2 tablespoons water, and the ⅛ teaspoon salt. Bring just to boiling on medium heat, stirring to dissolve brown sugar. Remove from heat.

⑤ Grease two 13 x 9 x 2-inch baking pans. Pour topping into prepared pans, spreading evenly. Sprinkle with pecans.

⑥ Punch dough down. Turn out onto a lightly floured surface. Divide in half. Cover and let rest for 10 minutes. Roll each portion of dough into a 15 x 10-inch rectangle. Spread each rectangle with 2 tablespoons of the softened butter. Sprinkle with filling, leaving about 1 inch unfilled along the long sides. Roll up each rectangle, starting from a filled long side; pinch dough to seal seams.

⑦ Slice each roll into 12 pieces. Place on top of pecan-sprinkled topping in pans. Cover and let rise in a warm place until nearly double in size (about 1 hour).

⑧ Preheat oven to 350°F. Bake for 25 to 30 minutes or until golden brown, covering with foil during the last 10 minutes if rolls are browning too quickly. Cool in pans on wire racks for 5 minutes; invert rolls onto baking sheets lined with parchment paper.

*Tip: To toast pecans, preheat oven to 350°F. Spread nuts in a shallow baking pan. Bake for 7 to 8 minutes or until golden brown, stirring once.

PER ROLL 375 calories; 17 g total fat (7 g sat. fat); 47 mg cholesterol; 300 mg sodium; 52 g carbohydrate; 2 g fiber; 6 g protein

Giant Cinnamon Rolls: Prepare as directed, except spread two-thirds of the topping in one 13 x 9 x 2-inch baking pan and one-third of the topping in one 8 x 1½-inch round baking pan. Cut 12 instead of 24 rolls; place 8 rolls in the 13 x 9-inch pan and 4 rolls in the 8-inch pan. Bake about 25 minutes or until golden brown, covering with foil during the last 10 minutes if rolls are browning too quickly.

Cream Cheese and Raspberry Coffee Cake

You can readily change the flavor of this time-honored recipe by substituting different fresh fruits—such as thinly sliced apricots or nectarines—for the raspberries. And when fresh fruit is out of season, use well-drained, thinly sliced canned apricots or peach slices instead.

MAKES 10 servings   **PREP** 20 minutes   **BAKE** 35 minutes   **COOL** 10 minutes   **OVEN** 375°F

Nonstick cooking spray
1¼   cups all-purpose flour
1¼   teaspoons baking powder
1   teaspoon finely shredded lemon or orange peel
¼   teaspoon baking soda
¼   teaspoon salt
1   cup granulated sugar
3   tablespoons butter, softened
¼   cup refrigerated or frozen egg product, thawed
1   teaspoon vanilla
½   cup buttermilk
2   ounces reduced-fat cream cheese (Neufchâtel)
2   tablespoons refrigerated or frozen egg product, thawed
1   cup fresh raspberries or frozen loose-pack raspberries
Powdered sugar
Fresh raspberries (optional)

① Preheat oven to 375°F. Lightly coat a 9 x 1½-inch round baking pan with cooking spray; set aside. In a medium bowl stir together flour, baking powder, lemon peel, baking soda, and salt.

② In a medium bowl beat ¾ cup of the granulated sugar and the butter with an electric mixer on medium to high until combined. Add the ¼ cup egg and vanilla. Beat on low to medium for 1 minute. Alternately add flour mixture and buttermilk to butter mixture, beating just until combined after each addition. Pour batter into the prepared baking pan, spreading evenly.

③ In a small bowl combine cream cheese and the remaining ¼ cup granulated sugar. Beat on medium to high until combined. Beat in the 2 tablespoons egg until combined. Sprinkle the 1 cup raspberries over batter in pan. Spoon cream cheese mixture over raspberries, allowing some of the berries to show.

④ Bake about 35 minutes or until a toothpick inserted near the center comes out clean. Cool in pan on a wire rack for 10 minutes. Sprinkle lightly with powdered sugar. Serve warm. If desired, garnish each serving with additional raspberries.

PER SERVING 195 calories; 5 g total fat (3 g sat. fat); 14 mg cholesterol; 223 mg sodium; 33 g carbohydrate; 1 g fiber; 4 g protein

Dried Cherry Scones

Scones are richer than ordinary biscuits because they often contain eggs, butter, and cream or sour cream.

MAKES 12 scones **PREP** 30 minutes **BAKE** 10 minutes
COOL 10 minutes **OVEN** 400°F

Boiling water
½ cup snipped dried sweet cherries or whole raisins
2 cups all-purpose flour
3 tablespoons packed brown sugar
2 teaspoons baking powder
½ teaspoon baking soda
½ teaspoon salt
¼ cup butter
1 teaspoon finely shredded orange peel
1 egg yolk, lightly beaten
1 8-ounce carton sour cream
1 cup powdered sugar
1 tablespoon orange juice
¼ teaspoon vanilla
Orange juice

① Preheat oven to 400°F. In a small bowl pour enough boiling water over dried cherries to cover. Let stand for 5 minutes; drain well. In a large bowl stir together flour, brown sugar, baking powder, baking soda, and salt. Using a pastry blender, cut in butter until mixture resembles coarse crumbs. Add drained cherries and orange peel; toss gently to coat. Make a well in the center of the flour mixture.

② In a small bowl combine egg yolk and sour cream. Add egg mixture all at once to flour mixture. Using a fork, stir until combined (mixture may seem dry).

③ Turn dough out onto a lightly floured surface. Knead dough by folding and gently pressing it for 10 to 12 strokes or until dough is nearly smooth. Pat or lightly roll dough into a 7-inch circle. Cut into 12 wedges.

④ Place wedges 1 inch apart on an ungreased baking sheet. Bake for 10 to 12 minutes or until light brown. Remove from baking sheet; cool on a wire rack for 10 minutes.

⑤ Meanwhile, for icing, in a small bowl stir together powdered sugar, the 1 tablespoon orange juice, and vanilla. Stir in enough additional orange juice to make an icing of drizzling consistency. Drizzle over warm scones.

PER SCONE 214 calories; 9 g total fat (4 g sat. fat); 31 mg cholesterol; 249 mg sodium; 32 g carbohydrate; 1 g fiber; 3 g protein

Blueberry Breakfast Scones

Nothing is finer in the morning than these warm, blueberry-studded scones drizzled with a sweet orange glaze.

MAKES 10 scones **PREP** 20 minutes
BAKE 15 minutes **OVEN** 400°F

2 cups all-purpose flour
¼ cup granulated sugar
1 tablespoon baking powder
1 tablespoon finely shredded orange peel
¼ teaspoon baking soda
¼ teaspoon salt
¼ cup butter
½ cup buttermilk or sour milk
¼ cup refrigerated or frozen egg product, thawed, or 1 egg
1 teaspoon vanilla
1 cup fresh or frozen blueberries
¾ cup powdered sugar
¼ teaspoon finely shredded orange peel
3 to 4 teaspoons orange juice or milk

① Preheat oven to 400°F. Lightly grease a baking sheet; set aside. In a large bowl stir together flour, granulated sugar, baking powder, the 1 tablespoon orange peel, baking soda, and salt. Using a pastry blender, cut in butter until mixture resembles coarse crumbs. Make a well in center of flour mixture. In a small bowl combine buttermilk, egg, and vanilla. Add egg mixture all at once to flour mixture. Stir just until moistened. Gently stir in blueberries.

② Turn dough out onto a lightly floured surface. Knead dough by folding and gently pressing for 12 to 15 strokes or until nearly smooth. On the prepared baking sheet pat or roll dough into a 7-inch circle. Cut dough into 10 wedges.

③ Bake for 15 to 20 minutes or until golden brown. Remove from baking sheet; cool on a wire rack.

④ For icing, in a small bowl stir together powdered sugar and the ¼ teaspoon orange peel. Stir in enough orange juice to make an icing of drizzling consistency. Drizzle over scones. Serve warm.

PER SCONE 194 calories; 5 g total fat (3 g sat. fat); 13 mg cholesterol; 273 mg sodium; 34 g carbohydrate; 1 g fiber; 4 g protein

Doughnut Muffins

Serve these cake doughnutlike muffins as a side to a main-dish salad or all alone for breakfast.

MAKES 12 muffins **PREP** 15 minutes **BAKE** 20 minutes **COOL** 5 minutes **OVEN** 350°F

½ **cup sugar**
⅓ **cup shortening**
1 **egg**
½ **teaspoon orange extract or vanilla**
1½ **cups all-purpose flour**
1½ **teaspoons baking powder**
½ **teaspoon salt**
½ **cup milk**
½ **cup sugar**
1 **teaspoon ground cinnamon**
¼ **cup butter, melted**

① Preheat oven to 350°F. Grease twelve 2½-inch muffin cups; set aside. In a large bowl combine ½ cup sugar and shortening. Beat with an electric mixer on medium to high until well mixed. Add egg and orange extract; beat well.

② In a small bowl stir together flour, baking powder, and salt. Alternately add flour mixture and milk to egg mixture, beating well after each addition. Spoon batter into the prepared muffin cups, filling each about two-thirds full.

③ Bake about 20 minutes or until a toothpick inserted in centers comes out clean. Cool in muffin cups on a wire rack for 5 minutes. Remove from muffin cups.

④ In a small bowl combine ½ cup sugar and cinnamon. While still warm, brush all sides of muffins with melted butter and dip into the cinnamon sugar. Serve warm.

PER MUFFIN 213 calories; 10 g total fat (4 g sat. fat); 29 mg cholesterol; 199 mg sodium; 28 g carbohydrate; 0 g fiber; 2 g protein

Cream Cheese-Pumpkin Muffins

These spiced muffins with coconut topping and cream cheese centers are first-rate for brunch.

MAKES 24 muffins **PREP** 30 minutes
BAKE 20 minutes **COOL** 5 minutes **OVEN** 375°F

- 1 8-ounce package cream cheese, softened
- 1 egg, lightly beaten
- 2 tablespoons sugar
- ⅔ cup flaked coconut
- ½ cup chopped walnuts or pecans
- 3 tablespoons sugar
- ½ teaspoon ground cinnamon
- 2¼ cups all-purpose flour
- 2 cups sugar
- 2 teaspoons baking powder
- 2 teaspoons ground cinnamon
- ½ teaspoon salt
- ¼ teaspoon baking soda
- 2 eggs, lightly beaten
- 1¼ cups canned pumpkin
- ¼ cup vegetable oil
- ½ teaspoon vanilla

① Preheat oven to 375°F. Grease twenty-four 2½-inch muffin cups or line with paper bake cups. Set aside.

② For filling, in a small bowl combine cream cheese, the 1 egg, and the 2 tablespoons sugar until smooth. For topping, in a small bowl stir together coconut, nuts, the 3 tablespoons sugar, and the ½ teaspoon cinnamon. Set aside.

③ In a large bowl stir together flour, the 2 cups sugar, baking powder, the 2 teaspoons cinnamon, salt, and baking soda. Make a well in the center of the flour mixture.

④ In a medium bowl combine 2 eggs, pumpkin, oil, and vanilla. Add egg mixture to flour mixture. Stir until moistened.

⑤ Spoon pumpkin batter into the muffin cups, filling each about one-third full. Drop a heaping teaspoon of the filling into each cup. Top with the remaining pumpkin batter, filling each cup about two-thirds full. Sprinkle with topping.

⑥ Bake for 20 to 25 minutes, or until a toothpick inserted near centers comes out clean. Cool in muffin cups on wire racks for 5 minutes. Remove from muffin cups.

PER MUFFIN 207 calories; 9 g total fat (3 g sat. fat); 37 mg cholesterol; 132 mg sodium; 30 g carbohydrate; 1 g fiber; 3 g protein

Breakfast Popovers

This dried cherry-dotted sweet bread resembles a cream puff. A light powdered sugar drizzle gives the popovers a snowy finish.

MAKES 24 popovers **PREP** 25 minutes
BAKE 30 minutes **OVEN** 375°F

- Boiling water
- ½ cup snipped dried cherries or whole raisins
- 1 cup water
- ½ cup butter
- 1 teaspoon granulated sugar
- ¼ teaspoon salt
- 1 cup all-purpose flour
- 4 eggs
- 4 teaspoons half-and-half or light cream
- 1 tablespoon butter, melted
- 1 teaspoon vanilla
- ¾ to 1 cup powdered sugar

① Preheat oven to 375°F. Grease 2 baking sheets; set aside. In a small bowl pour enough boiling water over dried cherries to cover. Set aside.

② In a medium saucepan combine the 1 cup water, the ½ cup butter, granulated sugar, and salt. Bring to boiling. Immediately add flour all at once; stir vigorously. Cook and stir until mixture forms a ball that doesn't separate. Remove from heat. Cool for 5 minutes.

③ Add eggs, 1 at a time, beating with a wooden spoon after each addition until smooth. Drain cherries; stir into batter.

④ Drop batter by tablespoons 1 inch apart onto the prepared baking sheets. Bake for 30 minutes. Transfer to wire racks; cool.

⑤ For glaze, in a small bowl combine half-and-half, the melted butter, and vanilla. Stir in enough powdered sugar to make a glaze of drizzling consistency. Drizzle over popovers.

PER POPOVER 94 calories; 5 g total fat (3 g sat. fat); 47 mg cholesterol; 68 mg sodium; 11 g carbohydrate; 0 g fiber; 2 g protein

Minted Fruit Compote

This treat gets marvelous flavor and color from assorted citrus, fresh mint, kiwifruit, and pomegranate seeds.

MAKES 6 servings **PREP** 25 minutes **CHILL** 2 to 24 hours

1   15.25-ounce can pineapple chunks (juice pack), undrained
2   tablespoons sugar
2   tablespoons snipped fresh mint or 1½ teaspoons dried mint, crushed
1   tablespoon finely slivered grapefruit peel
2   red grapefruits, peeled, halved lengthwise, and sliced ¼ inch thick
1   tablespoon finely slivered orange peel
2   oranges, peeled, halved lengthwise, and sliced ¼ inch thick
1   kiwifruit, peeled and sliced ¼ inch thick
¼   cup pomegranate seeds*
    Thin orange peel strips (optional)

① Drain pineapple, reserving juice; add enough water to juice to measure 1 cup liquid.

② For syrup, in a small saucepan combine the reserved 1 cup pineapple liquid, sugar, and mint. Bring just to boiling; reduce heat. Simmer, covered, for 5 minutes. Strain syrup, discarding mint. Cool slightly.

③ Meanwhile, in a large serving bowl combine pineapple, grapefruit peel, grapefruit slices, the slivered orange peel, orange slices, and kiwifruit slices. Pour strained syrup over fruit. Cover and chill for 2 to 24 hours.

④ Before serving, stir in pomegranate seeds. If desired, garnish with the orange peel strips.

*Tip: To remove pomegranate seeds, cut the fruit in half just through the skin. Remove the peel and break the fruit into sections. Then use your fingers or a small spoon to separate the seeds from the membrane. Handle the fruit in a bowl filled with water; this allows the seeds to float to the top, and the juice won't discolor your hands. Discard the skin and membrane, and eat only the seeds.

PER SERVING 98 calories; 0 g total fat; 0 mg cholesterol; 2 mg sodium; 25 g carbohydrate; 2 g fiber; 1 g protein

Gingered Melon

Enjoy this cool, refreshing melon cup for breakfast or dessert on the hottest days of summer.

MAKES 6 servings **PREP** 25 minutes **CHILL** 2 to 24 hours

¾   cup water
½   cup sugar
2   teaspoons finely shredded lemon peel (set aside)
4   teaspoons lemon juice
1½ to 2 teaspoons grated fresh ginger
4   cups watermelon, cantaloupe, and/or honeydew melon balls
⅓   cup flaked coconut

① For syrup, in a small saucepan combine the water, sugar, lemon juice, and ginger. Bring to boiling on medium heat; reduce heat. Simmer, uncovered, for 3 minutes. Remove from heat; stir in lemon peel. Cool to room temperature. If desired, strain syrup.

② Place melon balls in a medium bowl. Pour syrup over melon; stir gently to coat. Cover and chill for 2 to 24 hours.

③ To serve, spoon melon balls and syrup into dessert dishes. Sprinkle with coconut.

PER SERVING 122 calories; 2 g total fat (1 g sat. fat); 0 mg cholesterol; 10 mg sodium; 28 g carbohydrate; 1 g fiber; 1 g protein

Gingered Melon

Chapter 3

MEALS IN
MINUTES

Rely on these recipes to help you out of the what's-for-dinner jam.

Gingered Beef Stir-Fry

BEEF

Caprese Pasta
and Steak, 52

Corned Beef
Hash Patties, 58

Flank Steak with Parsley
and Lemon, 58

Gingered Beef Stir-Fry, 52

Grilled Steak and Plum
Pizzettes, 55

Smothered Steak with
Honeyed Red Onion, 56

Spinach and Basil Salad
with Beef, 57

LAMB

Rosemary
Lamb Chops, 59

PORK

Balsamic Pork Chops, 61

Ham and Swiss Skillet, 60

Pork and Papaya Salad, 59

CHICKEN AND TURKEY

Chicken Salad with Tahini
Dressing, 65

Ginger-Scented Honey-
Hoisin Chicken Thighs
with Sesame, 63

Pasta with Chicken,
Green Beans, and
Hazelnuts, 66

Pesto Chicken Breasts
with Summer Squash, 64

Tortilla Soup, 67

Zesty Skillet Turkey, 61

FISH AND SEAFOOD

Creamy Shrimp and
Spinach Stew, 69

Pepper Shrimp
in Peanut Sauce, 68

Warm Spinach
and Scallop Salad, 67

MEATLESS

Pasta with Broccoli
and Ginger, 70

Roma Tomato-Feta
Pasta, 70

Gingered Beef Stir-Fry

When you crave steak but not the high fat and calories, try this medley. Lean beef and crispy spring vegetables stir-fry together for a full-flavor dinner you can bring to the table in 25 minutes. (Pictured on page 50.)

MAKES 4 servings **START TO FINISH** 25 minutes

———————◆———————

8	ounces boneless beef top round steak
½	cup beef broth
3	tablespoons reduced-sodium soy sauce
2½	teaspoons cornstarch
1	teaspoon sugar
½	teaspoon grated fresh ginger
	Nonstick cooking spray
12	ounces asparagus, trimmed and cut diagonally into 1-inch pieces (2 cups)
1½	cups sliced fresh mushrooms
1	cup small broccoli florets
4	green onions, cut diagonally into 1-inch pieces
1	tablespoon vegetable oil
2	cups hot cooked rice

① Trim fat from meat. Thinly slice meat across the grain into bite-size strips. For sauce, in a small bowl stir together broth, soy sauce, cornstarch, sugar, and ginger. Set aside.

② Lightly coat a large skillet or wok with cooking spray; heat skillet on medium-high heat. Add asparagus, mushrooms, broccoli, and green onions; cook and stir for 3 to 4 minutes or until vegetables are crisp-tender. Remove vegetables from skillet.

③ Carefully add oil to hot skillet. Add meat; cook and stir for 2 to 3 minutes or until meat is slightly pink in center. Push meat from center of skillet. Stir sauce; add to center of skillet. Cook and stir until thickened and bubbly.

④ Return cooked vegetables to skillet; stir all ingredients together to coat with sauce. Cook and stir until heated through. Serve meat mixture with hot cooked rice.

PER SERVING 270 calories; 7 g total fat (2 g sat. fat); 36 mg cholesterol; 541 mg sodium; 32 g carbohydrate; 4 g fiber; 21 g protein

Caprese Pasta and Steak

The trio of fresh basil, roma tomatoes, and fresh mozzarella cheese is a traditional Italian flavor combo. Here it's used to dress up an easy pasta dish.

MAKES 4 servings **START TO FINISH** 30 minutes

———————◆———————

8	ounces dried large rigatoni pasta
1	pound boneless beef chuck top blade (flat-iron) steaks or bottom sirloin (tri-tip) steaks
½	cup basil pesto
4	roma tomatoes, sliced
4	ounces fresh mozzarella cheese, sliced
	Fresh basil leaves (optional)

① Cook pasta according to package directions; drain.

② Meanwhile, trim fat from meat. If necessary, cut meat into 4 serving-size pieces. Remove 2 tablespoons of the pesto; reserve the remaining pesto until ready to serve. Brush both sides of meat with the 2 tablespoons pesto. Heat a large heavy skillet on medium-high heat; add meat. Reduce heat to medium. Cook about 10 minutes for medium rare (145°F) to medium (160°F), turning once.

③ Divide cooked pasta among 4 dinner plates. Top with meat, tomatoes, and cheese.

④ Place the remaining pesto in a small microwave-safe bowl. Microwave on high about 20 seconds or until heated through, stirring once. Spoon some of the pesto over each serving. If desired, garnish with basil.

PER SERVING 695 calories; 35 g total fat (6 g sat. fat); 94 mg cholesterol; 486 mg sodium; 53 g carbohydrate; 3 g fiber; 40 g protein

Caprese Pasta and Steak

Grilled Steak and Plum Pizzettes

Ask Veronica Callaghan, a finalist in the 2009 National Beef Cook-Off, about her creative inspiration for Grilled Steak and Plum Pizzettes and it could be Plato's adage "Necessity is the mother of invention." With no stove or oven to use during a kitchen renovation, Veronica says she cooked everything on an outdoor grill, including pizza. She readily admits that working with bread dough can be a little tricky (and sticky) and advises you keep it well chilled and brush both sides of the dough circles with olive oil just before grilling.

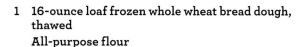

MAKES 4 pizzettes **PREP** 35 minutes **GRILL** 19 minutes

- 1 **16-ounce loaf frozen whole wheat bread dough, thawed**
   All-purpose flour
- 2 **medium firm, ripe red plums, each cut into 12 wedges**
- 2 **8-ounce boneless beef top loin steaks, cut 1 inch thick**
- ½ **teaspoon coarse black pepper**
- 1 **tablespoon olive oil**
   Salt
- ½ **cup crumbled blue cheese (2 ounces)**
- 2 **tablespoons coarsely chopped pistachio nuts**
- 2 **tablespoons honey**

① Divide bread dough into 4 portions. On a lightly floured surface, roll each portion into an 8- to 10-inch circle. If necessary, cover dough and let stand about 10 minutes so the dough rolls out easily. Layer dough circles between lightly floured sheets of waxed paper on a baking sheet; set aside.

② Thread plum wedges onto two 10- to 12-inch skewers,* leaving ¼ inch between pieces. Trim fat from meat. Sprinkle pepper evenly over meat; press in with your fingers.

③ For a charcoal grill, grill meat on the rack of an uncovered grill directly over medium coals for 10 to 12 minutes for medium rare (145°F) or 12 to 15 minutes for medium (160°F), turning once halfway through grilling. (For a gas grill, preheat grill. Reduce heat to medium. Place meat on grill rack over heat. Cover and grill as above.) While meat is grilling, add plum skewers to grill. Grill for 3 to 6 minutes or until plums are softened and starting to brown, turning once halfway through grilling. Remove meat and plum skewers from grill.

④ Brush both sides of dough circles with oil; add to grill. Grill, uncovered, for 4 to 6 minutes or until grill marks appear, turning once halfway through grilling. Remove crusts from grill.

⑤ Divide plum wedges among crusts. Cut meat into ¼-inch slices. Season with salt. Arrange meat on crusts; sprinkle with cheese and nuts.

⑥ Add pizzettes to grill. Cover and grill for 5 to 7 minutes or until cheese starts to melt. Drizzle with honey.

*Tip: If using wooden skewers, soak them in water for at least 30 minutes; drain before using.

PER PIZZETTE 756 calories; 32 g total fat (11 g sat. fat); 77 mg cholesterol; 1,071 mg sodium; 80 g carbohydrate; 6 g fiber; 42 g protein

Smothered Steak with Honeyed Red Onion

If you like, substitute a sweet onion variety, such as Vidalia or Walla Walla, for the red onion in the sweet-and-sour relish that tops these seared steaks.

MAKES 4 servings **START TO FINISH** 30 minutes

⅓   cup red wine vinegar

3   tablespoons honey

½   teaspoon dried thyme, crushed

1   large red onion, thinly sliced and separated into rings

1   pound boneless beef top loin steaks or tenderloin steaks, cut 1 inch thick

½   teaspoon cracked black pepper

2   tablespoons snipped fresh Italian (flat-leaf) parsley

① In a medium bowl combine vinegar, honey, and thyme. Add red onion, stirring to coat. Let stand while preparing the meat, stirring occasionally.

② Trim fat from meat. If necessary, cut meat into 4 serving-size pieces. Sprinkle pepper evenly over meat; press in with your fingers.

③ Heat a large nonstick skillet on medium-high heat. Add meat; cook for 10 minutes, turning once. Remove meat from skillet.

④ Add onion mixture to drippings in skillet. Cook on medium heat for 3 to 4 minutes or just until onion is crisp-tender, stirring occasionally.

⑤ Return meat and any accumulated juices to skillet. Cook on medium-low heat for 3 to 4 minutes for medium rare (145°F) to medium (160°F), occasionally spooning the cooking liquid over meat.

⑥ Transfer meat to 4 dinner plates. Spoon onion mixture onto meat and sprinkle with parsley.

PER SERVING 273 calories; 10 g total fat (4 g sat. fat); 76 mg cholesterol; 59 mg sodium; 19 g carbohydrate; 1 g fiber; 26 g protein

Spinach and Basil Salad with Beef

This beefy fresh spinach and basil salad owes its pleasing sweetness to the pear nectar that's used to make the dressing.

MAKES 4 servings **START TO FINISH** 25 minutes

¼ cup pear nectar
2 tablespoons canola oil
2 tablespoons white wine vinegar
½ teaspoon Worcestershire-style marinade for chicken
⅛ teaspoon freshly ground black pepper
4 cups fresh baby spinach
2 cups sliced fresh mushrooms
½ cup lightly packed fresh basil leaves
12 ounces cooked beef sirloin steak, cut into thin bite-size strips*
2 medium oranges, peeled and sectioned
¼ cup sliced almonds, toasted

① For dressing, in a screw-top jar combine pear nectar, oil, vinegar, Worcestershire-style marinade, and pepper. Cover and shake well.

② In a large bowl toss together spinach, mushrooms, and basil. Divide mixture among 4 dinner plates. Top with meat and oranges. Shake dressing again; drizzle over salads. Sprinkle with almonds.

*Tip: If you cook your meat, start with 1 to 1¼ pounds boneless beef top sirloin steak, cut 1 inch thick. Preheat broiler. Place meat on the unheated rack of a broiler pan. Broil 3 to 4 inches from the heat for 15 to 17 minutes for medium rare (145°F) or 20 to 22 minutes for medium (160°F), turning once halfway through broiling.

PER SERVING 311 calories; 15 g total fat (3 g sat. fat); 49 mg cholesterol; 92 mg sodium; 14 g carbohydrate; 4 g fiber; 30 g protein

Flank Steak with Parsley and Lemon

The drizzle of lemon-parsley sauce makes these strips of beef flank steak hard to resist.

MAKES 4 servings **START TO FINISH** 30 minutes

- 1 1¼- to 1½-pound beef flank steak
   Salt
   Freshly ground black pepper
- 4 teaspoons olive oil
- ¼ teaspoon finely shredded lemon peel
- 1 tablespoon lemon juice
- 1 tablespoon snipped fresh parsley
- 1 clove garlic, minced
- ¼ teaspoon salt
- ¼ teaspoon freshly ground black pepper
   Mashed New Potatoes (optional)

① Preheat broiler. Trim fat from meat. Lightly sprinkle both sides of meat with salt and pepper. Broil 3 to 4 inches from the heat for 17 to 21 minutes for medium (160°F), turning once halfway through broiling.

② Meanwhile, for sauce, in a small bowl whisk together oil, lemon peel, lemon juice, parsley, garlic, the ¼ teaspoon salt, and the ¼ teaspoon pepper.

③ Thinly slice meat diagonally across the grain. Transfer to a serving platter; drizzle with sauce. If desired, serve with Mashed New Potatoes.

Mashed New Potatoes: In a covered large saucepan cook 1½ pounds tiny new potatoes, quartered, in enough boiling salted water to cover about 15 minutes or until potatoes are fork-tender. Drain in a colander. In the same saucepan combine ¾ cup light (1%) milk, 2 tablespoons olive oil, ½ teaspoon salt, and ¼ teaspoon freshly ground black pepper. Heat until bubbles form around edge of pan. Return potatoes to saucepan; mash with a potato masher.

PER SERVING 263 calories; 14 g total fat (5 g sat. fat); 57 mg cholesterol; 367 mg sodium; 1 g carbohydrate; 0 g fiber; 30 g protein

Corned Beef Hash Patties

Start off with a breakfast built around these generous corned beef patties and you'll have what it takes to keep going all day.

MAKES 4 servings **START TO FINISH** 25 minutes

- 1½ cups shredded and coarsely chopped cooked corned beef brisket
- 3 medium potatoes, cooked, peeled, and coarsely shredded
- ½ cup chopped onion (1 medium)
- ½ teaspoon black pepper
- ½ cup butter

① In a large bowl combine corned beef, potatoes, onion, and pepper. Shape mixture into four 4-inch-diameter patties.

② In a very large skillet heat butter on medium heat until melted. Add patties; cook about 10 minutes or until golden brown, turning once.

PER SERVING 347 calories; 23 g total fat (11 g sat. fat); 88 mg cholesterol; 771 mg sodium; 23 g carbohydrate; 2 g fiber; 13 g protein

Rosemary Lamb Chops

If you use large shoulder chops, double the fresh rosemary mixture.

MAKES 4 servings **START TO FINISH** 20 minutes

—————◆—————

1	teaspoon finely snipped fresh rosemary
½	teaspoon salt
½	teaspoon black pepper
8	lamb rib chops or 4 lamb shoulder chops, cut 1 inch thick
1	tablespoon olive oil

① Preheat broiler. In a small bowl combine rosemary, salt, and pepper; set aside.

② Trim fat from chops. Brush both sides of chops with oil. Sprinkle with rosemary mixture. Broil 3 to 4 inches from the heat for 10 to 15 minutes for medium (160°F), turning once halfway through broiling.

PER SERVING 273 calories; 24 g total fat (10 g sat. fat); 57 mg cholesterol; 348 mg sodium; 0 g carbohydrate; 0 g fiber; 14 g protein

Pork and Papaya Salad

The orange-cilantro vinaigrette is the crowning flavor for this Caribbean-influenced salad made with black beans, garlic-rubbed pork, and papaya.

MAKES 4 servings **START TO FINISH** 30 minutes

————◆ • ◆————

3	tablespoons orange juice
3	tablespoons olive oil
2½	tablespoons snipped fresh cilantro
1	tablespoon rice wine vinegar
¼	teaspoon salt
1	15-ounce can black beans, rinsed and drained
1	to 1¼ pounds pork tenderloin
4	cloves garlic, minced
½	teaspoon salt
⅛	teaspoon freshly ground black pepper
1	ripe papaya, seeded, peeled, and sliced

① For dressing, in a small bowl combine orange juice, 2 tablespoons of the oil, the cilantro, vinegar, and the ¼ teaspoon salt. Transfer 1 tablespoon of the dressing to a medium bowl. Add beans; toss gently to coat. Set aside.

② Trim fat from meat. Cut meat into ¼-inch slices; transfer to another medium bowl. On a cutting board mash garlic, the ½ teaspoon salt, and the pepper together to form a paste. Using your hands, rub paste onto meat.

③ In a large nonstick skillet heat 1½ teaspoons of the oil on medium-high heat. Add half of the meat; cook about 4 minutes or until slightly pink in center, turning once. Remove from skillet. Repeat with the remaining 1½ teaspoons oil and the remaining meat.

④ To serve, spoon beans into the center of a serving platter. Arrange meat and papaya around beans. Drizzle with the remaining dressing.

PER SERVING 370 calories; 18 g total fat (4 g sat. fat); 85 mg cholesterol; 702 mg sodium; 21 g carbohydrate; 4 g fiber; 32 g protein

Ham and Swiss Skillet

You'll need to make this recipe in a broilerproof skillet so you can melt the cheese under the broiler.

MAKES 4 to 6 servings **START TO FINISH** 30 minutes

1	tablespoon butter or margarine
1	cup sliced fresh mushrooms
2	tablespoons sliced green onion (1)
¾	cup finely chopped zucchini
¾	cup finely chopped cooked ham
6	eggs
¼	teaspoon dried thyme, crushed
¼	teaspoon caraway seeds
	Dash salt
	Dash black pepper
½	cup shredded Swiss cheese (2 ounces)

① Preheat broiler. In a large nonstick or well-seasoned broilerproof skillet heat butter on medium-high heat until melted. Add mushrooms and green onion; cook about 5 minutes or until tender, stirring occasionally. Stir in zucchini. Cook, covered, on medium-low heat for 2 to 3 minutes or until crisp-tender, stirring occasionally. Stir in ham.

② In a medium bowl beat eggs until blended but not foamy. Stir in thyme, caraway seeds, salt, and pepper. Pour egg mixture over vegetable mixture in skillet.

③ Cook on medium heat. As mixture sets, run a spatula around edge of skillet, lifting egg mixture so uncooked portion flows underneath. Continue cooking and lifting edge until egg mixture is almost set (surface will be moist). Sprinkle with cheese.

④ Broil 4 to 5 inches from the heat for 1 to 2 minutes or just until top is set and cheese is melted. Cut into wedges.

PER SERVING 241 calories; 16 g total fat (7 g sat. fat); 355 mg cholesterol; 547 mg sodium; 3 g carbohydrate; 1 g fiber; 21 g protein

Balsamic Pork Chops

Today's lean pork chops cook fast, so don't walk away or the chops may overcook and be dry. Serve the chops with quick-cooking couscous and steamed broccoli.

MAKES 4 servings **START TO FINISH** 25 minutes

4	pork loin chops, cut 1 inch thick
	Salt
	Freshly ground black pepper
2	teaspoons olive oil
¼	cup finely chopped shallots (2 medium)
½	cup chicken broth
¼	cup balsamic vinegar
¼	teaspoon dried thyme, crushed
1	tablespoon butter or margarine

① Trim fat from chops. Sprinkle chops with salt and pepper. In a large skillet heat oil on medium-high heat. Add chops; cook about 10 minutes or until slightly pink in center and juices run clear (160°F), turning once. Transfer to a serving platter; cover loosely with foil and keep warm.

② For sauce, add shallots to drippings in skillet; cook and stir for 1 minute. Carefully add broth, vinegar, and thyme. Cook on high heat for 5 minutes, stirring frequently. Remove from heat; stir in butter. Serve chops with sauce.

PER SERVING 274 calories; 13 g total fat (5 g sat. fat); 91 mg cholesterol; 306 mg sodium; 5 g carbohydrate; 0 g fiber; 31 g protein

Zesty Skillet Turkey

If you enjoy spicy foods, you'll get a real kick out of this quick-cooking turkey main dish by opting for hot salsa.

MAKES 4 servings **START TO FINISH** 30 minutes

2	teaspoons olive oil
12	ounces turkey breast tenderloins, cut into 1-inch pieces
2	cloves garlic, minced
1	cup salsa
¼	cup raisins
1	tablespoon honey
¾	teaspoon ground cumin
½	teaspoon ground cinnamon
1	cup water
¼	teaspoon salt
¾	cup quick-cooking couscous
¼	cup slivered almonds, toasted

① In a large skillet heat oil on medium-high heat. Add turkey and garlic; cook and stir about 5 minutes or until turkey is no longer pink. Stir in salsa, raisins, honey, cumin, and cinnamon. Bring to boiling; reduce heat. Simmer, covered, for 5 minutes.

② Meanwhile, in a medium saucepan bring the water and salt to boiling. Stir in couscous. Remove from heat. Cover and let stand for 5 minutes. Fluff with a fork.

③ Serve turkey mixture over hot cooked couscous. Sprinkle with almonds.

PER SERVING 346 calories; 6 g total fat (1 g sat. fat); 53 mg cholesterol; 567 mg sodium; 44 g carbohydrate; 4 g fiber; 28 g protein

Ginger-Scented Honey-Hoisin Chicken Thighs with Sesame

This recipe, which was one of nine finalists in the 2009 National Chicken Cooking Contest sponsored by the National Chicken Council, is delicious, thrifty, quick, and easy—all admirable qualities. When coming up with this first-rate recipe, Ruth Kendrick of Ogden, Utah, confesses, "I like chicken thighs because they stay moist a lot longer and the meat has a much deeper and broader chicken flavor than breasts. They hold up well to the robust flavors of fresh ginger, soy sauce, and hoisin."

MAKES 4 servings **PREP** 25 minutes **BAKE** 10 minutes **OVEN** 325°F

1	tablespoon vegetable oil
8	skinless, boneless chicken thighs (1½ to 1¾ pounds total)
¼	cup soy sauce
¼	cup honey
¼	cup hoisin sauce
¼	cup chicken broth
1	to 2 tablespoons grated fresh ginger
½	teaspoon black pepper
¼	cup toasted sesame seeds
¼	cup sliced green onions (2)
4	cups hot cooked rice

① Preheat oven to 325°F. In a large oven-going skillet heat oil on medium-high heat. Add chicken; cook until brown on both sides. Drain off fat.

② Meanwhile, in a small saucepan combine soy sauce, honey, hoisin sauce, broth, ginger, and pepper. Bring to boiling; reduce heat. Simmer, uncovered, about 5 minutes or until mixture is slightly thickened.

③ Pour soy mixture over chicken in skillet, turning to coat. Bake for 10 to 15 minutes or until chicken is no longer pink (180°F).

④ Sprinkle chicken with sesame seeds and green onions. Serve with hot cooked rice.

PER SERVING 597 calories; 15 g total fat (3 g sat. fat); 142 mg cholesterol; 1,486 mg sodium; 73 g carbohydrate; 3 g fiber; 41 g protein

Pesto Chicken Breasts with Summer Squash

Using purchased pesto allows you to make this impressive chicken dish in just 20 minutes.

MAKES 4 servings   **START TO FINISH** 20 minutes

- **4** skinless, boneless chicken breast halves (about 12 ounces total)
  - Salt
  - Cracked black pepper
- **1** tablespoon olive oil
- **2** cups chopped zucchini and/or yellow summer squash (2 small)
- **2** tablespoons basil or dried tomato pesto
- **2** tablespoons finely shredded Asiago or Parmesan cheese

① Sprinkle chicken with salt and pepper. In a large nonstick skillet cook chicken in hot oil on medium heat for 4 minutes.

② Turn chicken; add zucchini and/or yellow squash. Cook for 4 to 6 minutes more or until chicken is no longer pink (170°F) and squash is crisp-tender, gently stirring squash once or twice.

③ Transfer chicken and squash to 4 dinner plates. Spoon pesto over chicken; sprinkle with cheese.

PER SERVING 186 calories; 10 g total fat (2 g sat. fat); 55 mg cholesterol; 129 mg sodium; 2 g carbohydrate; 1 g fiber; 23 g protein

Chicken Salad with Tahini Dressing

Tahini (tuh-HEE-nee), a thick paste made of ground sesame seeds, flavors the dressing for this refreshing chicken and bok choy salad. Look for it in the foreign foods section of your grocery store.

MAKES 4 servings **PREP** 15 minutes **BROIL** 12 minutes

12	ounces skinless, boneless chicken breast halves
¼	cup tahini (sesame seed paste)
3	tablespoons soy sauce
3	tablespoons red wine vinegar
2	tablespoons vegetable oil
2	teaspoons sugar
½	to 1 teaspoon chili oil or crushed red pepper
1	clove garlic, minced
1	to 2 tablespoons brewed tea, cooled, or water (optional)
4	to 6 cups shredded bok choy, romaine lettuce, or napa cabbage
2	small carrots, cut into thin bite-size strips
6	to 10 green onions, cut into thin bite-size strips
3	to 4 tablespoons peanuts

① Preheat broiler. Place chicken on the unheated rack of a broiler pan. Broil 4 to 5 inches from the heat for 12 to 15 minutes or until no longer pink (170°F), turning once halfway through broiling. Cut chicken into thin bite-size strips. Cover and chill until ready to serve.

② For dressing, in a small bowl stir together tahini, soy sauce, vinegar, oil, sugar, chili oil, and garlic. If necessary, thin with brewed tea.

③ To serve, divide bok choy among 4 dinner plates. Top with chicken, carrots, and green onions. Stir dressing again; drizzle over salads. Sprinkle with peanuts.

Make-Ahead Directions: Prepare dressing as directed. Cover and chill for up to 12 hours. Stir before serving.

PER SERVING 331 calories; 20 g total fat (2 g sat. fat); 49 mg cholesterol; 886 mg sodium; 13 g carbohydrate; 3 g fiber; 26 g protein

Pasta with Chicken, Green Beans, and Hazelnuts

There's nothing quite like the nutty goodness of toasted hazelnuts. To toast the nuts, simply spread them in a shallow baking pan and bake them in a 350°F oven for 10 to 12 minutes or until the skins crack. Wrap the hazelnuts in a kitchen towel and rub vigorously to remove the skins.

MAKES 6 servings **START TO FINISH** 30 minutes

1 pound dried ziti or penne pasta

2 tablespoons butter or margarine

1 pound green beans, trimmed and cut into 1-inch pieces

½ cup chicken broth

1 teaspoon salt

½ teaspoon freshly ground black pepper

⅔ cup whipping cream

2 cups thinly sliced cooked chicken

½ cup chopped toasted hazelnuts

① Cook pasta according to package directions; drain. Return pasta to hot pan; cover and keep warm.

② Meanwhile, in a large skillet heat butter on medium-high heat until melted. Add green beans; cook and stir for 2 minutes. Add broth, salt, and pepper. Bring to boiling; reduce heat. Cook, uncovered, for 5 minutes. Stir in cream. Cook, uncovered, about 5 minutes or until mixture is slightly thickened. Stir in cooked chicken; heat through.

③ Add chicken mixture and hazelnuts to cooked pasta; toss gently to coat.

PER SERVING 591 calories; 25 g total fat (10 g sat. fat); 88 mg cholesterol; 554 mg sodium; 65 g carbohydrate; 6 g fiber; 27 g protein

Tortilla Soup

Anaheims or poblanos add a lively beat to corn and fresh tomatoes in this aromatic meal in a bowl.

MAKES 6 servings **START TO FINISH** 30 minutes

- 2 to 4 Anaheim or poblano chiles, seeded and chopped*
- 1 cup chopped onion (1 large)
- 1 tablespoon cumin seeds
- 4 cloves garlic, minced
- 2 tablespoons vegetable oil
- 2 14-ounce cans reduced-sodium chicken broth
- 1½ cups fresh or frozen whole kernel corn
- 1½ cups chopped tomatoes (3 medium)
- 1½ cups coarsely shredded cooked chicken
- ½ cup snipped fresh cilantro
- 2 cups coarsely crushed tortilla chips
- 1 cup shredded Monterey Jack cheese (4 ounces) (optional)
  Tortilla chips (optional)
  Lime wedges (optional)
  Fresh cilantro sprigs (optional)

① In a large Dutch oven cook chiles, onion, cumin seeds, and garlic in hot oil on medium heat about 5 minutes or until onion is tender, stirring occasionally. Add broth, corn, tomatoes, chicken, and the snipped cilantro. Bring to boiling; reduce heat. Simmer, covered, for 10 minutes.

② To serve, divide the 2 cups crushed tortilla chips among 6 soup bowls. Ladle soup on top of crushed chips. If desired, sprinkle each serving with cheese and garnish with additional tortilla chips, lime wedges, and the cilantro sprigs.

*Tip: Because chiles contain volatile oils that can burn your skin and eyes, avoid direct contact with them as much as possible. When working with chiles, wear plastic or rubber gloves. If your bare hands do touch the peppers, wash your hand and nails well with soap and warm water.

PER SERVING 274 calories; 13 g total fat (2 g sat. fat); 29 mg cholesterol; 504 mg sodium; 26 g carbohydrate; 4 g fiber; 16 g protein

Warm Spinach and Scallop Salad

This warm blend of mixed greens, tender scallops, and crunchy nuts is refreshing on a cool day.

MAKES 4 servings **START TO FINISH** 25 minutes

- 12 ounces fresh or frozen bay scallops
- 4 cups torn fresh spinach leaves
- 4 cups torn butterhead (Boston or bibb) lettuce
- ½ cup sweet red pepper strips
- ¼ cup shredded carrot
- 3 tablespoons water
- 2 tablespoons lemon juice
- 2 tablespoons honey
- 1 tablespoon yellow mustard
- 2 tablespoons vegetable oil
- 2 tablespoons finely chopped shallot (1 medium)
- ¼ cup chopped pecans, toasted

① Thaw scallops, if frozen. Rinse scallops; pat dry with paper towels. Set aside. In a large salad bowl combine spinach, lettuce, sweet pepper, and carrot.

② For dressing, in a screw-top jar combine the water, lemon juice, honey, and mustard. Cover and shake well.

③ In a large skillet heat oil on medium-high heat. Add scallops and shallot. Cook and stir for 1 to 3 minutes or until scallops are opaque. Using a slotted spoon, transfer scallop mixture to spinach mixture.

④ Shake dressing again; pour into skillet. Bring just to boiling. Pour dressing over spinach mixture; toss gently to coat. Sprinkle with pecans. Serve immediately.

PER SERVING 198 calories; 14 g total fat (1 g sat. fat); 25 mg cholesterol; 228 mg sodium; 17 g carbohydrate; 4 g fiber; 14 g protein

Pepper Shrimp in Peanut Sauce

Who could resist this shrimp and pasta stir-fry? A sweet and spicy peanut sauce dresses up whimsical bow tie pasta that's served with colorful and crisp sweet peppers, green onions, and best of all, shrimp.

MAKES 4 servings **START TO FINISH** 30 minutes

1	pound fresh or frozen shrimp in shells
8	ounces dried bow tie pasta or linguine or 1 cup uncooked long grain rice
½	cup water
¼	cup orange marmalade
2	tablespoons peanut butter
2	tablespoons soy sauce
2	teaspoons cornstarch
¼	teaspoon crushed red pepper
1	tablespoon vegetable oil
2	cups sweet red and/or orange pepper strips (2 medium)
6	green onions, cut diagonally into 1-inch pieces
	Chopped peanuts (optional)

① Thaw shrimp, if frozen. Peel and devein shrimp. Rinse shrimp; pat dry with paper towels. Set aside. In a 4-quart Dutch oven cook pasta according to package directions; drain. Return pasta to hot pan; cover and keep warm.

② Meanwhile, for sauce, in a small bowl stir together the water, marmalade, peanut butter, soy sauce, cornstarch, and crushed red pepper. Set aside.

③ Pour oil into a wok or large skillet; heat on medium-high heat. (Add more oil as necessary during cooking.) Add sweet peppers and onions; cook and stir for 1 to 2 minutes or until crisp-tender. Remove vegetables from wok.

④ Add half of the shrimp to wok; cook and stir for 2 to 3 minutes or until shrimp are opaque; remove from wok. Repeat with the remaining shrimp.

⑤ Stir sauce; add to wok. Cook and stir until thickened and bubbly. Cook and stir for 2 minutes more. Remove from heat; keep sauce warm.

⑥ Add vegetables and shrimp to cooked pasta. Cook on medium heat until heated through, tossing gently to combine. Serve shrimp mixture on 4 dinner plates. Top with warm sauce. If desired, sprinkle with peanuts.

PER SERVING 497 calories; 11 g total fat (2 g sat. fat); 172 mg cholesterol; 685 mg sodium; 66 g carbohydrate; 5 g fiber; 35 g protein

Creamy Shrimp and Spinach Stew

A bit of nutmeg brings out the best in the shrimp and emphasizes the slightly sweet, nutty taste of the Gruyère cheese.

MAKES 4 servings **START TO FINISH** 30 minutes

---

0   ounces fresh or frozen peeled and deveined small shrimp
1   cup sliced fresh mushrooms
½   cup chopped onion (1 medium)
1   clove garlic, minced
2   tablespoons butter
3   tablespoons all-purpose flour
1   bay leaf
⅛   teaspoon ground nutmeg
⅛   teaspoon black pepper
1   14-ounce can vegetable broth or chicken broth
1   cup half-and-half, light cream, or milk
2   cups torn fresh spinach leaves
¾   cup shredded Gruyère cheese (3 ounces)

① Thaw shrimp, if frozen. Rinse shrimp; pat dry with paper towels. Set aside.

② In a medium saucepan cook mushrooms, onion, and garlic in hot butter on medium heat until tender. Stir in flour, bay leaf, nutmeg, and pepper. Add broth and half-and-half all at once.

③ Cook and stir until mixture is thickened and bubbly. Add shrimp. Cook and stir for 2 minutes more. Add spinach and cheese. Cook and stir just until spinach is wilted and cheese is melted. Remove and discard bay leaf.

PER SERVING 322 calories; 21 g total fat (12 g sat. fat); 147 mg cholesterol; 617 mg sodium; 12 g carbohydrate; 2 g fiber; 22 g protein

Pasta with Broccoli and Ginger

This quick and easy pasta sauce is made with broccoli stems pureed in chicken broth (so it really coats the pasta) as well as bite-size florets, for a dish that's green and fresh-tasting with a pleasing hint of aromatic ginger.

MAKES 6 servings **START TO FINISH** 30 minutes

1 pound dried fusilli, rotelle, or radiatore pasta
1 bunch broccoli (1½ pounds)
½ cup chicken broth
2 tablespoons olive oil
1 tablespoon minced fresh ginger
2 cloves garlic, minced
⅛ to ¼ teaspoon crushed red pepper
1 cup chicken broth
½ teaspoon salt

① Cook pasta according to package directions; drain. Return pasta to hot pan; cover and keep warm.

② Meanwhile, cut broccoli florets from stems; trim into small florets. Peel and slice stems. In a food processor combine sliced stems and the ½ cup broth. Cover and process until broccoli is finely chopped.

③ In a large skillet heat oil on medium-high heat. Add ginger, garlic, and crushed red pepper; cook and stir for 15 seconds. Stir in broccoli florets, pureed broccoli stems, the 1 cup broth, and salt. Bring to boiling; reduce heat. Cook for 5 to 8 minutes or just until broccoli is tender, stirring occasionally. Pour broccoli mixture over cooked pasta; toss gently to coat.

PER SERVING 350 calories; 6 g total fat (1 g sat. fat); 1 mg cholesterol; 462 mg sodium; 62 g carbohydrate; 4 g fiber; 12 g protein

Roma Tomato-Feta Pasta

The flavors of fresh-from-the-garden tomatoes, onion, and parsley mingle while the pasta cooks. Then feta cheese adds a final flavor boost.

MAKES 6 servings **START TO FINISH** 25 minutes

1 pound dried radiatore or corkscrew pasta
3 cups chopped roma tomatoes
½ cup chopped red onion (1 medium)
⅓ cup snipped fresh parsley
3 tablespoons olive oil
½ teaspoon salt
½ teaspoon freshly ground black pepper
2 cups crumbled feta cheese (8 ounces)

① Cook pasta according to package directions; drain. Return pasta to hot pan; cover and keep warm.

② Meanwhile, in a large bowl combine tomatoes, red onion, parsley, oil, salt, and pepper. Add cooked pasta and cheese; toss gently to combine.

PER SERVING 462 calories; 16 g total fat (7 g sat. fat); 34 mg cholesterol; 625 mg sodium; 63 g carbohydrate; 4 g fiber; 16 g protein

Roma Tomato-Feta Pasta

Chapter 4

COOK IT SLOWLY

Slow-cooking is the next best thing to having someone cook for you.

Cajun Pot Roast

BEEF

Cajun Pot Roast, 74

Country Swiss Steak, 75

PORK

Cherry-Cola Ham, 79

Pulled Pork Sandwiches
with Root Beer
Barbecue Sauce, 78

Ribs with Apple and
Sauerkraut, 76

Tuscan Ham and
Bean Soup, 80

LAMB

Moroccan Lamb
and Fruit Stew, 81

CHICKEN AND TURKEY

Chicken and Shrimp
Jambalaya, 85

Easy Chicken
Tetrazzini, 82

Hoisin-Sauced
Turkey Tenderloin, 86

MEATLESS

Chunky
Vegetable Chili, 75

Mushroom Goulash, 88

Pasta with
Lentil Sauce, 89

Saucy Multigrain
Spaghetti
with Tofu, 90

Cajun Pot Roast

Cajun seasoning and Cajun-style tomatoes make this beef pot roast a true bayou-style meal. For even more Cajun flavor serve some cooked okra alongside. (Pictured on page 72.)

MAKES 6 servings **PREP** 25 minutes **COOK** 10 to 12 hours (low) or 5 to 6 hours (high)

- 1   2- to 2½-pound boneless beef chuck pot roast
- 2   to 3 teaspoons Cajun seasoning or Homemade Cajun Seasoning
- 1   tablespoon vegetable oil
- 1   14.5-ounce can Cajun-style or Mexican-style stewed tomatoes, undrained
- 1   cup chopped onion (1 large)
- 1   cup chopped celery (2 stalks)
- ¼   cup quick-cooking tapioca
- 2   cloves garlic, minced
- 3   cups hot cooked rice

① Trim fat from meat. If necessary, cut meat to fit into a 3½- or 4-quart slow cooker. Sprinkle both sides of meat with Cajun seasoning; rub in with your fingers. In a large skillet cook meat in hot oil on medium-high heat until brown on all sides. Drain off fat.

② In the slow cooker combine tomatoes, onion, celery, tapioca, and garlic. Place meat on top of tomato mixture.

③ Cover and cook on low-heat setting for 10 to 12 hours or on high-heat setting for 5 to 6 hours.

④ Remove meat from cooker. Slice meat. Serve meat and tomato mixture over hot cooked rice.

PER SERVING 273 calories; 7 g total fat (2 g sat. fat); 55 mg cholesterol; 366 mg sodium; 31 g carbohydrate; 2 g fiber; 21 g protein

Homemade Cajun Seasoning: In a small bowl combine ½ teaspoon white pepper, ½ teaspoon garlic powder, ½ teaspoon onion powder, ½ teaspoon paprika, ½ teaspoon black pepper, and ¼ to ½ teaspoon cayenne pepper.

Chunky Vegetable Chili

To tame the hotness of this meatless chili, use regular stewed tomatoes and a mild salsa. If you like, counteract the heat even more with warm corn bread muffins.

MAKES 4 servings **PREP** 15 minutes
COOK 8 to 10 hours (low) or 4 to 5 hours (high)

———————◆———————

1   medium zucchini, quartered lengthwise and cut into ½-inch pieces (1½ cups)
1   cup coarsely chopped sweet green pepper
½   cup coarsely chopped onion (1 medium)
½   cup coarsely chopped celery (1 stalk)
2   to 3 teaspoons chili powder
2   cloves garlic, minced
1   teaspoon dried oregano, crushed
½   teaspoon ground cumin
2   14.5-ounce cans Mexican-style stewed tomatoes, undrained
1   15.25-ounce can whole kernel corn, undrained
1   15-ounce can black beans, rinsed and drained
1   8-ounce jar salsa
    Sour cream

① In a 3½- or 4-quart slow cooker combine zucchini, sweet pepper, onion, celery, chili powder, garlic, oregano, and cumin. Stir in tomatoes, corn, beans, and salsa.

② Cover and cook on low-heat setting for 8 to 10 hours or on high-heat setting for 4 to 5 hours. Top each serving with sour cream.

PER SERVING 274 calories; 4 g total fat (1 g sat. fat); 6 mg cholesterol; 1,405 mg sodium; 52 g carbohydrate; 14 g fiber; 13 g protein

Country Swiss Steak

The Swiss don't actually make Swiss steak. The recipe name is believed to be English and likely comes from relating the process of smoothing out cloth between rollers, called "swissing," to the pounding and flattening of meat, a step skipped in this slow cooker version.

MAKES 4 servings **PREP** 15 minutes
COOK 10 to 12 hours (low)

———————◆———————

1   pound boneless beef round steak, cut 1 inch thick
4   ounces uncooked spicy bratwurst or other sausage, cut into ¾-inch slices
1   tablespoon vegetable oil
1   small onion, sliced and separated into rings
2   tablespoons quick-cooking tapioca
1   teaspoon dried thyme, crushed
¼   teaspoon salt
¼   teaspoon black pepper
1   14.5-ounce can diced tomatoes with basil, garlic, and oregano, undrained
2   cups hot cooked noodles or rice
    Fresh thyme sprigs (optional)

① Trim fat from beef. Cut beef into 4 serving-size pieces. In a large skillet cook beef and sausage in hot oil on medium-high heat until brown on both sides. Drain off fat.

② Place onion in a 3½- or 4-quart slow cooker. Sprinkle with tapioca, the dried thyme, salt, and pepper. Pour tomatoes over onion. Add beef and sausage.

③ Cover and cook on low-heat setting for 10 to 12 hours. Serve meat mixture with hot cooked noodles. If desired, garnish with the fresh thyme.

PER SERVING 460 calories; 20 g total fat (6 g sat. fat); 109 mg cholesterol; 996 mg sodium; 36 g carbohydrate; 2 g fiber; 34 g protein

Ribs with Apple and Sauerkraut

Quick browning in a skillet seals in the natural juices of the country-style ribs, adding sensational flavor and aroma.

MAKES 4 servings **PREP** 30 minutes **COOK** 8 to 10 hours (low) or 4 to 5 hours (high)

2½ pounds pork country-style ribs, halved crosswise and cut into 1- or 2-rib portions

1 tablespoon vegetable oil

2 medium potatoes, sliced ½ inch thick

2 medium carrots, sliced ¼ inch thick

1 medium onion, thinly sliced

1 8-ounce can (about 1 cup) sauerkraut, rinsed and drained

½ cup apple cider or apple juice

2 teaspoons caraway seeds or fennel seeds

⅛ teaspoon ground cloves

2 tablespoons cold water

1 tablespoon all-purpose flour

½ of a large apple, cored and thinly sliced
   Salt (optional)
   Black pepper (optional)

1 tablespoon snipped fresh Italian (flat-leaf) parsley

① In a large skillet cook ribs in hot oil on medium-high heat until brown on both sides. Drain off fat.

② In a 3½- or 4-quart slow cooker combine potatoes, carrots, and onion. Top with ribs and sauerkraut. In a small bowl combine cider, caraway seeds, and cloves. Pour over sauerkraut.

③ Cover and cook on low-heat setting for 8 to 10 hours or on high-heat setting for 4 to 5 hours. Using a slotted spoon, transfer ribs and vegetables to a serving platter; cover and keep warm.

④ For gravy, strain cooking liquid into a glass measuring cup. Skim off fat. Measure 1 cup liquid (if necessary, add water); pour into a small saucepan. In a small bowl combine the water and flour; stir into liquid in saucepan. Cook and stir on medium heat until thickened and bubbly. Stir in apple. Cook and stir for 1 minute more. If desired, season to taste with salt and pepper.

⑤ Serve ribs and vegetables with gravy. Sprinkle with parsley.

PER SERVING 431 calories; 20 g total fat (7 g sat. fat); 103 mg cholesterol; 371 mg sodium; 32 g carbohydrate; 4 g fiber; 31 g protein

Pulled Pork Sandwiches with Root Beer Barbecue Sauce

Root beer adds a slight sweetness to the barbecue sauce for these zesty pulled pork sandwiches.

MAKES 8 to 10 servings **PREP** 25 minutes **COOK** 8 to 10 hours (low) or 4 to 5 hours (high)

1 2½- to 3-pound boneless pork sirloin roast
½ teaspoon salt
½ teaspoon black pepper
1 tablespoon vegetable oil
2 medium onions, cut into thin wedges
1 cup root beer*
6 cloves garlic, minced
3 cups root beer* (two 12-ounce cans or bottles)
1 cup chili sauce
¼ teaspoon root beer concentrate (optional)
6 to 8 dashes bottled hot pepper sauce (optional)
8 to 10 hamburger buns, split (toasted, if desired)
   Lettuce leaves (optional)
   Tomato slices (optional)

① Trim fat from meat. If necessary, cut meat to fit into a 3½- to 5-quart slow cooker. Sprinkle meat with salt and pepper.

② In a large skillet cook meat in hot oil on medium-high heat until brown on all sides. Drain off fat. Transfer meat to the cooker. Add onions, the 1 cup root beer, and garlic.

③ Cover and cook on low-heat setting for 8 to 10 hours or on high-heat setting for 4 to 5 hours.

④ Meanwhile, for sauce, in a medium saucepan combine the 3 cups root beer and chili sauce. Bring to boiling; reduce heat. Boil gently, uncovered, about 30 minutes or until mixture is reduced to 2 cups, stirring occasionally. If desired, stir in root beer concentrate and hot pepper sauce.

⑤ Transfer meat to a serving platter. Using 2 forks, pull meat apart into shreds. Using a slotted spoon, transfer onions to platter. Discard cooking liquid.

⑥ If desired, line bottoms of buns with lettuce and tomato. Add shredded meat and onions; drizzle with sauce. Replace tops of buns.

*Tip: Do not use diet root beer.

PER SERVING 433 calories; 12 g total fat (3 g sat. fat); 89 mg cholesterol; 877 mg sodium; 45 g carbohydrate; 3 g fiber; 35 g protein

Cherry-Cola Ham

Cherry-flavor cola makes this moist brown sugar-glazed ham delightfully sweet and tangy.

MAKES 20 to 24 servings **PREP** 20 minutes **COOK** 8 to 9 hours (low)

1 cup packed brown sugar
⅔ cup cherry-flavor cola
2 tablespoons lemon juice
1 tablespoon dry mustard
1 5- to 5½-pound cooked boneless ham
¼ cup cold water
2 tablespoons cornstarch
1 tablespoon prepared horseradish
  Fresh sage leaves (optional)

① In a 5½- or 6-quart slow cooker combine brown sugar, cola, lemon juice, and dry mustard. Add ham, turning to coat. Cover and cook on low-heat setting for 8 to 9 hours. Transfer ham to a serving platter; cover and keep warm.

② For sauce, in a small saucepan stir together the water and cornstarch. Add cooking liquid from cooker. Cook and stir on medium heat until thickened and bubbly. Cook and stir for 2 minutes more. Stir in horseradish.

③ Slice ham. Serve ham with sauce. If desired, garnish with sage.

PER SERVING 201 calories; 7 g total fat (2 g sat. fat); 81 mg cholesterol; 1,379 mg sodium; 13 g carbohydrate; 0 g fiber; 20 g protein

Tuscan Ham and Bean Soup

This long-simmering soup gets a dose of fresh flavor when you add kale or spinach just before serving.

MAKES 8 servings **PREP** 25 minutes **COOK** 6 to 8 hours (low) or 3 to 4 hours (high)

3	15-ounce cans small white beans, rinsed and drained
2½	cups cubed cooked ham
1½	cups sliced carrots (3 medium)
1	cup sliced celery (2 stalks)
1	cup chopped onion (1 large)
¼	teaspoon black pepper
2	14.5-ounce cans diced tomatoes with basil, garlic, and oregano, undrained
2	14-ounce cans reduced-sodium chicken broth
8	cups torn fresh kale or spinach leaves
	Freshly shredded Parmesan cheese (optional)

① In a 5- to 6-quart slow cooker stir together beans, ham, carrots, celery, onion, and pepper. Stir in tomatoes and broth.

② Cover and cook on low-heat setting for 6 to 8 hours or on high-heat setting for 3 to 4 hours.

③ Before serving, stir in kale. If desired, sprinkle each serving with cheese.

PER SERVING 323 calories; 3 g total fat (1 g sat. fat); 21 mg cholesterol; 2,099 mg sodium; 53 g carbohydrate; 12 g fiber; 25 g protein

Moroccan Lamb and Fruit Stew

A flavorful mix of spices teams with dried apricots and dates to provide an exotic, spicy-sweet taste. Serve the stew with couscous, a tiny semolina grain that's a staple in North African cuisine.

MAKES 6 to 8 servings **PREP** 30 minutes **COOK** 7 to 9 hours (low) or 3½ to 4½ hours (high) + 30 minutes (high)

- 2 pounds boneless leg of lamb or beef bottom round roast
- 1 to 2 teaspoons crushed red pepper
- ¾ teaspoon ground turmeric
- ¾ teaspoon ground ginger
- ¾ teaspoon ground cinnamon
- ½ teaspoon salt
- 2 tablespoons olive oil or vegetable oil
- 2 cups chopped onions (2 large)
- 3 cloves garlic, minced
- 1 14-ounce can beef broth
- 2 tablespoons cold water
- 1 tablespoon cornstarch
- 1 cup pitted whole dates
- 1 cup dried apricots
- 3 to 4 cups hot cooked couscous or rice
- ¼ cup toasted slivered almonds
  Orange peel curls (optional)

① Trim fat from meat. Cut meat into 1- to 1½-inch pieces. In a plastic bag combine crushed red pepper, turmeric, ginger, cinnamon, and salt. Add meat pieces, a few at a time, shaking to coat.

② In a large skillet cook meat, one-third at a time, in hot oil on medium-high heat until brown. Drain off fat. Transfer meat to a 3½- or 4-quart slow cooker. Stir in onions and garlic. Pour broth over mixture in cooker.

③ Cover and cook on low-heat setting for 7 to 9 hours or on high-heat setting for 3½ to 4½ hours or until meat is tender. Skim off fat.

④ In a small bowl combine the water and cornstarch; stir into meat mixture. Stir in dates and apricots. If using low-heat setting, turn to high-heat setting. Cover and cook about 30 minutes more or until mixture is slightly thickened and bubbly.

⑤ To serve, ladle meat mixture over hot cooked couscous. Sprinkle with almonds and, if desired, orange peel curls.

PER SERVING 500 calories; 12 g total fat (2 g sat. fat); 95 mg cholesterol; 541 mg sodium; 62 g carbohydrate; 7 g fiber; 38 g protein

Easy Chicken Tetrazzini

Legend has it that Chicken Tetrazzini was created for a famous opera singer—but that doesn't stop this dish from being wonderfully homey, crowd-pleasing fare!

MAKES 8 servings **PREP** 20 minutes **COOK** 5 to 6 hours (low) or 2½ to 3 hours (high)

2½   pounds skinless, boneless chicken breast halves and/or thighs, cut into 1-inch pieces

2   4-ounce cans (drained weight) sliced mushrooms, drained

1   16-ounce jar Alfredo pasta sauce

¼   cup chicken broth or water

2   tablespoons dry sherry (optional)

¼   teaspoon ground nutmeg

¼   teaspoon black pepper

10   ounces dried spaghetti or linguine

⅔   cup grated Parmesan cheese

¾   cup diagonally sliced green onions (6)
     Toasted French bread slices (optional)

① In a 3½- or 4-quart slow cooker combine chicken and mushrooms. In a medium bowl combine pasta sauce, broth, sherry (if desired), nutmeg, and pepper. Pour over mixture in cooker.

② Cover and cook on low-heat setting for 5 to 6 hours or on high-heat setting for 2½ to 3 hours.

③ Before serving, cook spaghetti according to package directions; drain. Stir cheese into chicken mixture in cooker. Serve chicken mixture over hot cooked spaghetti. Sprinkle each serving with green onions. If desired, serve with French bread.

PER SERVING 430 calories; 14 g total fat (6 g sat. fat); 121 mg cholesterol; 753 mg sodium; 32 g carbohydrate; 2 g fiber; 42 g protein

Chicken and Shrimp Jambalaya

If you like spicy food, use Homemade Cajun Seasoning. The Cajun seasoning blend you buy at the supermarket is less peppery than this home-mixed three-pepper combo.

MAKES 6 servings **PREP** 20 minutes **COOK** 5 to 6 hours (low) or 2½ to 3 hours (high) **STAND** 10 minutes

---

1 **14.5-ounce can diced tomatoes, undrained**
1 **14-ounce can reduced-sodium chicken broth**
1 **cup sliced celery (2 stalks)**
1 **cup chopped onion (1 large)**
½ **of a 6-ounce can (⅓ cup) tomato paste**
1 **tablespoon Worcestershire sauce**
1½ **teaspoons Cajun seasoning or Homemade Cajun Seasoning**
1 **pound skinless, boneless chicken breast halves or thighs, cut into ¾-inch pieces**
8 **ounces fresh or frozen peeled and deveined cooked shrimp**
1½ **cups uncooked instant rice**
¾ **cup chopped sweet green pepper (1 medium)**

① In a 3½- or 4-quart slow cooker combine tomatoes, broth, celery, onion, tomato paste, Worcestershire sauce, and Cajun seasoning. Stir in chicken.

② Cover and cook on low-heat setting for 5 to 6 hours or on high-heat setting for 2½ to 3 hours.

③ Before serving, thaw shrimp, if frozen. Stir shrimp, rice, and sweet pepper into chicken mixture. Let stand, covered, for 10 to 15 minutes or until rice is tender and most of the liquid is absorbed.

PER SERVING 259 calories; 2 g total fat (0 g sat. fat); 117 mg cholesterol; 634 mg sodium; 30 g carbohydrate; 3 g fiber; 30 g protein

Homemade Cajun Seasoning: In a small bowl combine ½ teaspoon white pepper, ½ teaspoon garlic powder, ½ teaspoon onion powder, ½ teaspoon paprika, ½ teaspoon black pepper, and ¼ to ½ teaspoon cayenne pepper.

Hoisin-Sauced Turkey Tenderloin

If the turkey breast tenderloin you find at the supermarket is larger than 8 ounces, trim the tenderloin and freeze the remaining turkey for another meal.

MAKES 2 servings **PREP** 20 minutes **COOK** 3 to 4 hours (low) or 1½ to 2 hours (high)

½   **cup sweet red pepper strips**
½   **of a small onion, cut into thin wedges**
8   **ounces turkey breast tenderloin, halved crosswise**
1   **clove garlic, minced**
⅛   **teaspoon salt**
⅛   **teaspoon black pepper**
2   **tablespoons orange juice**
2   **tablespoons hoisin sauce**
¾   **cup uncooked instant brown rice**
2   **tablespoons sliced green onion (1) (optional)**
1   **tablespoon sliced almonds, toasted (optional)**

① In a 1½-quart slow cooker combine sweet pepper strips and onion wedges. Place turkey on top of vegetables. Sprinkle with garlic, salt, and black pepper. In a small bowl combine orange juice and hoisin sauce; pour over mixture in cooker.

② Cover and cook on low-heat setting for 3 to 4 hours or on high-heat setting for 1½ to 2 hours. If no heat setting is available, cook for 2 to 3 hours.

③ Before serving, cook rice according to package directions, omitting any salt and butter.

④ Slice turkey. Serve turkey and vegetable mixture with hot cooked rice. If desired, sprinkle with the green onion and almonds.

PER SERVING 325 calories; 5 g total fat (1 g sat. fat); 68 mg cholesterol; 408 mg sodium; 37 g carbohydrate; 4 g fiber; 32 g protein

Mushroom Goulash

Goulash is typically a meaty dish well-seasoned with paprika and served with noodles. This caraway-accented variation substitutes portobello mushrooms for the meat.

MAKES 6 servings **PREP** 25 minutes **COOK** 8 to 9 hours (low) or 4 to 4½ hours (high)

16	ounces fresh baby portobello mushrooms, sliced
1	tablespoon dried minced onion
3	cloves garlic, minced
1	14.5-ounce can no-salt-added diced tomatoes, undrained
1	14-ounce can vegetable broth
1	6-ounce can no-salt-added tomato paste
2	tablespoons paprika
1	teaspoon dried oregano, crushed
1	teaspoon caraway seeds
¼	teaspoon salt
¼	teaspoon black pepper
8	ounces dried egg noodles
½	cup light sour cream

① In a 3½- or 4-quart slow cooker combine mushrooms, dried onion, and garlic. Stir in tomatoes, broth, tomato paste, paprika, oregano, caraway seeds, salt, and pepper.

② Cover and cook on low-heat setting for 8 to 9 hours or on high-heat setting for 4 to 4½ hours.

③ Before serving, cook noodles according to package directions; drain. Stir sour cream into mushroom mixture in cooker. Serve mushroom mixture over hot cooked noodles.

PER SERVING 251 calories; 5 g total fat (2 g sat. fat); 43 mg cholesterol; 443 mg sodium; 43 g carbohydrate; 5 g fiber; 12 g protein

Pasta with Lentil Sauce

Lentils share the flavor spotlight with onion, carrots, and celery in this meatless slow-simmered pasta sauce.

MAKES 8 servings **PREP** 15 minutes **COOK** 12 to 14 hours (low) or 6 to 7 hours (high)

1 26- to 28-ounce jar meatless tomato-base pasta sauce
1 14-ounce can vegetable broth
½ cup water
1 cup brown or yellow lentils, rinsed and drained
1 cup chopped onion (1 large)
1 cup chopped carrots (2 medium)
1 cup chopped celery (2 stalks)
¼ teaspoon crushed red pepper
4 cups hot cooked penne pasta
    Finely shredded Parmesan cheese (optional)

① In a 4½- or 5-quart slow cooker combine pasta sauce, broth, and the water. Stir in lentils, onion, carrots, celery, and crushed red pepper.

② Cover and cook on low-heat setting for 12 to 14 hours or on high-heat setting for 6 to 7 hours.

③ Serve lentil mixture over hot cooked pasta. If desired, sprinkle each serving with cheese.

PER SERVING 404 calories; 4 g total fat (1 g sat. fat); 0 mg cholesterol; 667 mg sodium; 75 g carbohydrate; 12 g fiber; 16 g protein

Saucy Multigrain Spaghetti with Tofu

Looking for a tasty way to add soy to your diet? Try this Italian-style one-dish meal that gets its protein from tofu.

MAKES 8 servings **PREP** 20 minutes **COOK** 7 to 8 hours (low) or 3½ to 4 hours (high)

---

2 14.5-ounce cans no-salt-added diced tomatoes, undrained
1 10.75-ounce can reduced-fat and reduced-sodium condensed cream of mushroom soup
2 cups sliced carrots (4 medium)
1½ cups sliced celery (3 stalks)
1½ cups chopped onions (3 medium)
4 cloves garlic, minced
2 teaspoons dried Italian seasoning, crushed
½ teaspoon salt
¼ teaspoon black pepper
8 ounces dried multigrain spaghetti, broken
1 16-ounce package extra-firm tub-style tofu (fresh bean curd), drained and cubed
½ cup shredded reduced-fat cheddar cheese (2 ounces)

① In a 3½- or 4-quart slow cooker stir together tomatoes and soup. Stir in carrots, celery, onions, garlic, Italian seasoning, salt, and pepper.

② Cover and cook on low-heat setting for 7 to 8 hours or on high-heat setting for 3½ to 4 hours.

③ Before serving, cook spaghetti according to package directions; drain. Gently stir cooked spaghetti and tofu into tomato mixture. Sprinkle each serving with cheese.

PER SERVING 212 calories; 4 g total fat (1 g sat. fat); 5 mg cholesterol; 464 mg sodium; 32 g carbohydrate; 5 g fiber; 13 g protein

Chapter 5

GREAT
GRILLING

Tuck into the smoky flavor of flame-grilled meats, fish, and chicken.

Mediterranean Burgers

BEEF

Grilled Flank Steak
and Onions, 96

Herb Cheese-Stuffed
Steaks, 97

Sizzling Steak and
Peaches, 94

Skirt Steak Fajitas
with Grilled Onions
and Peppers, 95

Stay-Awake Steak, 96

Tri-Tip Steaks with
Texas Toast, 98

BISON

Smoky Barbecued
Bison Burgers, 99

PORK AND LAMB

Brats with
Mango Relish, 100

Honey-Glazed Creole
Pork Tenderloin with
Jambalaya Stuffing, 103

Mediterranean
Burgers, 100

CHICKEN

Polynesian Honey-
Pineapple Chicken, 110

Southwest Grilled
Chicken, 111

Spicy Chipotle Chicken
Spears, 109

FISH AND SEAFOOD

Grilled Salmon
with Tomato-Ginger
Relish, 104

Marinated Tuna
Steaks, 107

Port-Glazed Grilled
Salmon with Basil-Peach
Relish, 106

Sesame Salmon
with Asian Slaw, 104

Shrimp with Sweet
Pepper Relish, 107

Sizzling Steak and Peaches

Add freshly ground black pepper to these open-face sandwiches to give them a peppery kick. For the best peach sauce, make sure your peaches are ripe enough to get that wonderful sweet sugary flavor.

MAKES 4 servings **PREP** 30 minutes **GRILL** 10 minutes

Tangy Peach Sauce
4   slices thick-sliced bacon, cut crosswise into thirds
4   6-ounce boneless beef shoulder top blade (flat-iron), ribeye, or top loin steaks, cut 1 inch thick
    Salt
    Freshly ground black pepper
2   peaches, halved lengthwise
4   slices Texas toast, toasted

① Prepare Tangy Peach Sauce. Remove ½ cup of the sauce for basting. Set aside the remaining sauce until ready to serve.

② In a large skillet cook bacon on medium heat until crisp. Remove bacon and drain on paper towels. Trim fat from steaks. Sprinkle steaks with salt and pepper.

③ For a charcoal grill, grill steaks on the rack of an uncovered grill directly over medium coals for 10 to 12 minutes for medium rare (145°F) or 12 to 15 minutes for medium (160°F), turning once halfway through grilling and brushing with the reserved ½ cup sauce during the last 5 minutes of grilling. (For a gas grill, preheat grill. Reduce heat to medium. Place steaks on grill rack over heat. Cover and grill as above.)

④ While steaks are grilling, add peach halves to grill. Grill about 3 minutes or until peaches are heated through and light brown, turning once halfway through grilling. Cut each peach half into 4 wedges.

⑤ To serve, place toast slices on dinner plates. Top with bacon, steaks, and grilled peach wedges. Pass the remaining sauce.

Tangy Peach Sauce: In a food processor combine 2 cups peeled and sliced peaches (2 medium), ¼ cup peach nectar, 2 tablespoons condensed beef broth, 2 tablespoons balsamic vinegar, 1 tablespoon packed brown sugar, 1 tablespoon finely chopped onion, and ¼ teaspoon ground cinnamon. Cover and process until nearly smooth. Transfer

mixture to a small saucepan. Bring to boiling; reduce heat. Simmer, uncovered, about 10 minutes or until mixture reaches desired consistency, stirring occasionally. Makes about 1 cup.

PER SERVING 690 calories; 16 g total fat (6 g sat. fat); 88 mg cholesterol; 840 mg sodium; 87 g carbohydrate; 7 g fiber; 47 g protein

Skirt Steak Fajitas with Grilled Onions and Peppers

Enjoy Tex-Mex fajitas for dinner tonight. Wrap garlic-seasoned strips of grilled skirt steak with grilled sweet peppers and onions in warm flour tortillas for tempting, stick-to-the-ribs roll-ups.

MAKES 8 servings **PREP** 35 minutes **MARINATE** 1 hour **GRILL** 14 minutes

---

2	pounds beef skirt steak
4	cloves garlic, minced
¾	teaspoon salt
¾	cup lime juice
¼	cup vegetable oil
2	tablespoons chili powder
2	tablespoons ground cumin
¼	teaspoon black pepper
3	large sweet red peppers
12	large green onions
16	6- to 7-inch flour tortillas
	Sour cream
	Refrigerated avocado dip (guacamole) (optional)

① Trim fat from meat. Place meat in a large resealable plastic bag set in a shallow dish.

② For marinade, on a cutting board mash garlic and salt together to form a paste. In a small bowl combine garlic paste, lime juice, 2 tablespoons of the oil, the chili powder, cumin, and black pepper. Pour marinade over meat. Seal bag; turn to coat meat. Marinate in the refrigerator for 1 hour, turning bag once or twice.

③ Halve sweet peppers lengthwise; remove stems, seeds, and membranes. Trim green onions. Brush sweet peppers and onions with the remaining 2 tablespoons oil. Stack tortillas and wrap tightly in foil.

④ For a charcoal grill, place sweet peppers, green onions, and tortilla packet on the rack of an uncovered grill directly over medium-hot coals. (Be sure to lay green onions perpendicular to the grill grates so they won't fall into the coals.) Grill until peppers are light brown, onions are just tender, and tortillas are warm, turning occasionally to cook evenly. Allow 8 to 12 minutes for peppers, 4 to 5 minutes for onions, and about 10 minutes for tortillas. (For a gas grill, preheat grill. Reduce heat to medium-high. Place peppers, onions, and tortilla packet on grill rack over heat. Cover and grill as above.) Transfer peppers and onions to a bowl; cover and keep warm. Remove tortillas from grill.

⑤ Drain meat, discarding marinade. Add meat to grill. Grill about 4 minutes or until slightly pink in center, turning once halfway through grilling. Remove from grill. Thinly slice meat diagonally across the grain. Coarsely chop peppers and onions.

⑥ Fill warm tortillas with meat, peppers, and onions. Top with sour cream and, if desired, avocado dip. Fold tortillas in half or roll up tortillas.

PER SERVING 588 calories; 32 g total fat (10 g sat. fat); 81 mg cholesterol; 748 mg sodium; 43 g carbohydrate; 5 g fiber; 30 g protein

Grilled Flank Steak and Onions

This bold marinade made with balsamic vinegar and Dijon mustard is a quick way to flavor lamb or chicken as well as beef.

MAKES 5 servings **PREP** 15 minutes
MARINATE 15 minutes **GRILL** 10 minutes

◆━━━●━━━◆

1¼ pounds beef flank steak
¼ cup balsamic vinegar
2 teaspoons Dijon mustard
1 teaspoon salt
1 teaspoon dried rosemary, crushed
1 teaspoon olive oil
3 medium onions, cut into ½-inch slices

① Trim fat from meat. For marinade, in a large shallow glass dish combine vinegar, mustard, salt, rosemary, and oil. Add meat and onions, turning to coat. Cover and marinate at room temperature for 15 minutes. Drain meat and onions, reserving marinade.

② For a charcoal grill, grill meat and onions on the rack of an uncovered grill directly over medium* coals for 10 to 14 minutes for medium rare (145°F) or 17 to 21 minutes for medium (160°F), turning and brushing once with marinade halfway through grilling. (For a gas grill, preheat grill. Reduce heat to medium. Place meat and onions on grill rack over heat. Cover and grill as above.) Discard any remaining marinade.

③ Slice meat diagonally across the grain. Serve meat with onions.

*Tip: To test for medium coals, you should be able to hold your hand over the coals at the height of the food for 4 seconds before you have to pull away.

PER SERVING 222 calories; 9 g total fat (4 g sat. fat); 40 mg cholesterol; 578 mg sodium; 8 g carbohydrate; 1 g fiber; 25 g protein

Stay-Awake Steak

You've heard of camp coffee—the kind cowboys enjoyed around the fire with a good, fresh steak. Somebody put the two together, and the result is this toasty-tasting piece of beef.

MAKES 6 servings **PREP** 15 minutes
MARINATE 2 to 24 hours **GRILL** 22 minutes

◆━━━●━━━◆

1½ pounds boneless beef top sirloin steak, cut 1 inch thick
½ cup chopped onion (1 medium)
½ cup steak sauce or hickory-flavor barbecue sauce
¼ to ⅓ cup brewed espresso or strong coffee
2 tablespoons Worcestershire sauce
2 cups hickory, pecan, or oak wood chips
2 12-ounce cans beer or 3 cups water

① Trim fat from meat. Place meat in a resealable plastic bag set in a shallow dish. For marinade, in a small bowl combine onion, steak sauce, espresso, and Worcestershire sauce. Pour marinade over meat. Seal bag; turn to coat meat. Marinate in the refrigerator for 2 to 24 hours, turning bag occasionally. Drain meat, discarding marinade.

② At least 1 hour before grilling, soak wood chips in beer. Drain before using.

③ For a charcoal grill, arrange medium-hot coals around a drip pan. Test for medium heat above pan. Sprinkle drained wood chips over coals. Place meat on grill rack over drip pan. Cover and grill for 22 to 26 minutes for medium rare (145°F) or 26 to 30 minutes for medium (160°F). (For a gas grill, preheat grill. Reduce heat to medium. Adjust for indirect cooking. Add drained wood chips according to the manufacturer's directions. Place meat on grill rack over burner that is off. Grill as above.)

④ To serve, thinly slice meat across the grain.

PER SERVING 251 calories; 17 g total fat (7 g sat. fat); 74 mg cholesterol; 138 mg sodium; 2 g carbohydrate; 0 g fiber; 22 g protein

Herb Cheese-Stuffed Steaks

Here's a beef lover's delight—tender beef tenderloin stuffed with roasted sweet peppers and herb-flavor cheese grilled to perfection and served with a roasted sweet pepper sauce and mellow, roasted garlic on a stick.

MAKES 6 servings **PREP** 25 minutes **GRILL** 10 minutes

---

6   beef tenderloin steaks, cut 1 inch thick

1   12-ounce jar roasted sweet red peppers, drained

1   5.2-ounce container semisoft cheese with garlic and herbs

12   fresh basil leaves, torn

¼   cup bottled red wine vinaigrette salad dressing

¼   teaspoon salt

¼   teaspoon black pepper

1   green onion, cut up

1   tablespoon snipped fresh basil

3   cloves garlic, quartered

    Roasted Garlic Skewers (optional)

①   Trim fat from steaks. Make a pocket in each steak by cutting horizontally from a long side to within ½ inch of each of the other sides.

②   For stuffing, coarsely chop enough of the roasted sweet peppers to make ⅓ cup; reserve the remaining peppers for sauce. In a small bowl combine the ⅓ cup coarsely chopped peppers, cheese, and the torn basil. Spoon stuffing into pockets in steaks. If necessary, secure openings with wooden toothpicks. Brush steaks with 2 tablespoons of the vinaigrette dressing; reserve the remaining dressing for sauce. Sprinkle steaks with salt and black pepper.

③   For a charcoal grill, grill steaks on the rack of an uncovered grill directly over medium coals for 10 to 12 minutes for medium rare (145°F) or 12 to 15 minutes for medium (160°F), turning once halfway through grilling. (For a gas grill, preheat grill. Reduce heat to medium. Place steaks on grill rack over heat. Cover and grill as above.)

④   Meanwhile, for sauce, in a food processor or blender combine the reserved roasted sweet peppers, green onion, the snipped basil, and garlic. Cover and process or blend until chopped. Transfer to a serving bowl. Stir in the reserved vinaigrette dressing.

⑤   Remove and discard any toothpicks from steaks. Serve steaks with sauce and, if desired, Roasted Garlic Skewers.

PER SERVING 602 calories; 46 g total fat (19 g sat. fat); 147 mg cholesterol; 353 mg sodium; 5 g carbohydrate; 1 g fiber; 39 g protein

Roasted Garlic Skewers: Preheat oven to 425°F. Divide 1 whole garlic bulb into individual cloves; peel cloves and cut in half lengthwise. Place garlic cloves in a custard cup. Drizzle with 1 teaspoon olive oil. Cover with foil and roast about 20 minutes or until garlic feels soft. When cool enough to handle, thread garlic cloves onto skewers.* Add garlic skewers to the grill during the last 5 minutes of grilling, turning once halfway through grilling.

*Tip: If using wooden skewers, soak them in water for at least 30 minutes; drain before using.

Tri-Tip Steaks with Texas Toast

A molasses-bourbon marinade and sauce flavors this spicy meat, which is served on Texas toast and heaped with shredded romaine, slivered red onion, and pickled jalapeño slices. If Texas toast is unavailable, buy an unsliced loaf of bread and cut extra-thick slices.

MAKES 6 to 8 servings   **PREP** 30 minutes   **MARINATE** 2 to 3 hours   **GRILL** 17 minutes

1½	to 2 pounds boneless beef bottom sirloin (tri-tip) steaks, cut 1 inch thick
⅔	cup bourbon
⅓	cup reduced-sodium soy sauce
¼	cup molasses
2	tablespoons cider vinegar
2	teaspoons chili powder
½	cup ketchup
½	cup water
6	tablespoons butter, softened
¼	teaspoon black pepper
1	tablespoon vegetable oil
6	to 8 slices Texas toast
	Shredded romaine lettuce (optional)
	Slivered red onion (optional)
	Pickled jalapeño slices (optional)

① Trim fat from meat. Place meat in a resealable plastic bag set in a shallow dish. For marinade, in a small bowl combine bourbon, soy sauce, molasses, vinegar, and chili powder. Remove ¼ cup of the marinade for sauce. Pour the remaining marinade over meat. Seal bag; turn to coat meat. Marinate in the refrigerator for 2 to 3 hours, turning bag occasionally.

② For sauce, in a small saucepan combine the reserved ¼ cup marinade, ketchup, the water, 2 tablespoons of the butter, and the pepper. Bring to boiling on medium heat. Set aside.

③ Drain meat, discarding marinade. Brush both sides of meat with oil.

④ For a charcoal grill, arrange medium-hot coals on one side of grill. Place meat on grill rack directly over coals. Cover and grill about 4 minutes or until meat is light brown, turning once halfway through grilling. Move meat to unheated side of grill. Cover and grill for 12 to 15 minutes more for medium rare (145°F). (For a gas grill, preheat grill. Reduce heat to medium-high. Adjust for indirect cooking. Grill as above, starting meat over burner that is on and finishing meat over burner that is off.) Remove meat from grill.

⑤ Spread bread with the remaining 4 tablespoons butter. Add bread to grill. Grill for 1 to 2 minutes or until bread is toasted.

⑥ To serve, reheat sauce. Thinly slice meat. Arrange meat slices on toast; spoon sauce over meat. If desired, top with lettuce, red onion, and jalapeño.

Tip: The tri-tip—a triangular-shape cut of beef from the bottom sirloin primal cut—is lean, tender, full of flavor, and relatively inexpensive. If you prefer to cut your own steaks, purchase a 1½- to 2-pound boneless beef bottom sirloin (tri-tip) roast and slice it into 1-inch steaks.

PER SERVING 513 calories; 27 g total fat (11 g sat. fat); 169 mg cholesterol; 970 mg sodium; 31 g carbohydrate; 1 g fiber; 35 g protein

Smoky Barbecued Bison Burgers

It's hard to decide what's best about this adventurous grilled sandwich—the tangy mayonnaise sauce perked up with barbecue sauce, dill pickle, and horseradish or the plump bison burgers accented with Gouda cheese and Dijon mustard.

MAKES 4 servings **PREP** 25 minutes **GRILL** 14 minutes

¼	cup mayonnaise
2	tablespoons barbecue sauce
1	tablespoon chopped dill pickle
2	teaspoons prepared horseradish
1	cup shredded smoked Gouda cheese (4 ounces)
1	tablespoon country Dijon mustard
4	cloves garlic, minced
2	teaspoons smoked paprika
½	teaspoon black pepper
¼	teaspoon salt
1½	pounds ground bison (buffalo)
4	whole grain hamburger buns, split and toasted
	Tomato slices
	Red onion slices

① For sauce, in a small bowl combine mayonnaise, 1 tablespoon of the barbecue sauce, the pickle, and horseradish. Cover and chill until ready to serve.

② In a large bowl combine the remaining 1 tablespoon barbecue sauce, cheese, mustard, garlic, paprika, pepper, and salt. Add ground bison; mix well, but do not overmix. Shape mixture into four ¾-inch-thick patties.

③ For a charcoal grill, grill patties on the greased rack of an uncovered grill directly over medium coals for 14 to 16 minutes or until done (160°F), turning once halfway through grilling. (For a gas grill, preheat grill. Reduce heat to medium. Place patties on greased grill rack over heat. Cover and grill as above.)

④ Spread bottoms of buns with sauce. Add burgers, tomato, and red onion. Replace tops of buns.

PER SERVING 550 calories; 30 g total fat (11 g sat. fat); 111 mg cholesterol; 1,187 mg sodium; 30 g carbohydrate; 3 g fiber; 40 g protein

Mediterranean Burgers

Lamb, cucumber, feta cheese, and fresh mint add a whole new world of flavor to the tried-and-true burger. Biting into one of these patties is like taking a mini trip to Greece. (Pictured on page 92.)

MAKES 4 servings **PREP** 15 minutes **GRILL** 14 minutes

———◆———

1	pound lean ground lamb or beef
2	teaspoons freshly ground black pepper
4	kaiser rolls, split and toasted
4	lettuce leaves
4	tomato slices
½	cup thinly sliced cucumber
½	cup crumbled feta cheese (2 ounces)
1	tablespoon snipped fresh mint

① Shape ground meat into four ¾-inch-thick patties. Sprinkle pepper evenly over patties; press in with your fingers.

② For a charcoal grill, grill patties on the rack of an uncovered grill directly over medium coals for 14 to 18 minutes or until done (160°F), turning once halfway through grilling. (For a gas grill, preheat grill. Reduce heat to medium. Place patties on grill rack over heat. Cover and grill as above.)

③ Line bottoms of rolls with lettuce. Top with burgers, tomato, cucumber, cheese, and mint; replace tops of rolls.

PER SERVING 435 calories; 21 g total fat (9 g sat. fat); 88 mg cholesterol; 535 mg sodium; 33 g carbohydrate; 1 g fiber; 28 g protein

Brats with Mango Relish

This delightful grilled mango relish flavored with jerk seasoning makes your taste buds tingle. It takes brats hot off the grill to new flavor heights.

MAKES 4 servings **START TO FINISH** 20 minutes

———◆———

1	large mango, halved lengthwise, seeded, and peeled
1	small red onion, cut into ½-inch slices
3	tablespoons vegetable oil
4	cooked smoked bratwurst (12 ounces total)
2	hearts of romaine lettuce, halved
½	teaspoon Jamaican jerk seasoning
	Salt
	Black pepper
4	hoagie buns, bratwurst buns, or other crusty rolls, split and toasted

① Brush mango and red onion with 1 tablespoon of the oil.

② For a charcoal grill, grill mango, onion, and bratwurst on the rack of an uncovered grill directly over medium coals about 8 minutes or until mango and brats are brown and heated through and onion is crisp-tender, turning once halfway through grilling. (For a gas grill, preheat grill. Reduce heat to medium. Place mango, onion, and bratwurst on grill rack over heat. Cover and grill as above.)

③ Meanwhile, lightly brush lettuce with 1 tablespoon of the oil. While brats are grilling, add lettuce to grill. Grill for 1 to 2 minutes or until light brown and wilted, turning once halfway through grilling.

④ For mango relish, chop grilled mango and onion. In a medium bowl combine mango, onion, the remaining 1 tablespoon oil, and jerk seasoning. Season to taste with salt and pepper. Serve brats in buns with mango relish. Serve lettuce on the side.

PER SERVING 671 calories; 38 g total fat (10 g sat. fat); 50 mg cholesterol; 1,397 mg sodium; 67 g carbohydrate; 5 g fiber; 18 g protein

Brats with Mango Relish

Honey-Glazed Creole Pork Tenderloin with Jambalaya Stuffing

Adding flavor and flair to meals is Glenn Lyman's passion. When this Charlotte, North Carolina, chef entered his Grilled Honey-Glazed Creole Pork Tenderloin with Jambalaya Stuffing in the Sur La Table Grilling Recipe Contest, he was in it to win it. His tongue-tingling recipe was Grand-Prize Winner in the Grilled Meat Entrée category that was judged by Steven Raichlen, grilling cookbook author and host of Primal Grill *on PBS.*

MAKES 8 servings **PREP** 1 hour **GRILL** 30 minutes **STAND** 10 minutes

---

8 ounces fresh or frozen medium shrimp in shells
2 tablespoons olive oil
1 cup chopped onion (1 large)
½ cup chopped sweet green pepper (1 small)
½ cup chopped celery (1 stalk)
8 ounces cooked smoked sausage (such as andouille or kielbasa), quartered lengthwise and cut into ½-inch pieces
3 bay leaves
6 cloves garlic, minced
1 14.5-ounce can diced tomatoes, undrained
2 teaspoons Creole seasoning
1 teaspoon kosher salt
1 cup uncooked long grain white rice
¼ cup chopped green onions (2)
2 1-pound pork tenderloins
  Fresh thyme sprigs
  Creole seasoning
  Olive oil
2 tablespoons honey
2 tablespoons butter, melted
1½ teaspoons Creole or Dijon mustard
  Snipped fresh parsley and/or chopped green onions (optional)

① For stuffing, thaw shrimp, if frozen. Peel, devein, and rinse shrimp; pat dry with paper towels. In a 4- to 5-quart Dutch oven heat the 2 tablespoons oil on medium heat. Add onion, sweet pepper, and celery; cook for 4 to 5 minutes or until vegetables begin to soften, stirring occasionally.

② Add sausage and bay leaves; cook for 2 minutes. Add shrimp and garlic; cook about 2 minutes or until shrimp are opaque. Stir in tomatoes, the 2 teaspoons Creole seasoning, and salt. Cook for 5 minutes, stirring frequently.

③ Stir in rice. Simmer, covered, for 20 to 25 minutes or until rice is tender and liquid is absorbed. Remove from heat. Let stand, covered, for 5 minutes. Remove and discard bay leaves. Stir in the ¼ cup green onions. Cool.

④ Trim fat from tenderloins. Make a lengthwise cut down the center of each tenderloin, cutting almost to, but not through, the opposite side. Spread open. Place each tenderloin between 2 pieces of plastic wrap. Using the flat side of a meat mallet, pound into a ½-inch-thick rectangle.

⑤ Spread 1 cup stuffing over each rectangle. Bring up long sides of rectangle around stuffing, overlapping edges. Tie at 2-inch intervals with 100%-cotton kitchen string. Place remaining stuffing in a disposable foil pan and cover with foil.

⑥ Tuck thyme sprigs under the string on tenderloins. Sprinkle with additional Creole seasoning and drizzle with additional oil. For glaze, in a small bowl combine honey, melted butter, and mustard.

⑦ For a charcoal grill, arrange medium-hot coals around a drip pan. Test for medium heat above pan. Place tenderloins on grill rack directly over coals. Grill about 5 minutes or until meat is brown, giving meat a quarter turn once halfway through grilling. Turn tenderloins over and move to indirect heat over drip pan. Place pan of stuffing next to tenderloins directly over coals. Cover and grill for 25 to 30 minutes or until an instant-read thermometer inserted into meat registers 155°F, brushing once with glaze halfway through grilling. (For a gas grill, preheat grill. Reduce heat to medium. Adjust for indirect cooking. Grill as above.)

⑧ Remove tenderloins and stuffing from grill. Cover tenderloins with foil; let stand for 10 minutes. Slice each tenderloin into 4 pieces. Serve with stuffing. If desired, garnish with parsley and/or additional green onions.

Make-Ahead Directions: Prepare stuffing through Step 3, but transfer to a nonreactive bowl or a baking sheet lined with plastic wrap before cooling. Cover; chill up to 24 hours.

PER SERVING 455 calories; 21 g total fat (7 g sat. fat); 142 mg cholesterol; 948 mg sodium; 29 g carbohydrate; 2 g fiber; 35 g protein

Grilled Salmon with Tomato-Ginger Relish

Freshly grated ginger adds unexpected sweetness and heat to the red and yellow cherry tomato combo.

MAKES 8 to 10 servings **PREP** 20 minutes
GRILL 13 minutes per fillet

———◆———

- 6   cups red and/or yellow cherry tomatoes, finely chopped
- 3   tablespoons white balsamic vinegar or white wine vinegar
- 1   tablespoon grated fresh ginger
- 1   teaspoon salt
- 2   3- to 3½-pound fresh or frozen whole salmon fillets with skin
- 1   tablespoon olive oil
- 1   teaspoon salt
- ½   teaspoon freshly ground black pepper
- 3   tablespoons fresh thyme leaves
     Fresh thyme sprigs (optional)
     Lime wedges (optional)

① For relish, in a medium bowl combine tomatoes, vinegar, ginger, and 1 teaspoon salt. Set aside.

② Thaw fish, if frozen. Rinse fish; pat dry with paper towels. Brush both sides of fish with oil. Sprinkle with 1 teaspoon salt and pepper. Sprinkle the thyme leaves on skinned sides of fish; press gently with your fingers.

③ For a charcoal grill, grill 1 of the fish fillets, skin side up, on the rack of an uncovered grill directly over medium coals for 8 to 10 minutes or until light brown. Using 2 large metal spatulas, carefully turn fish. Grill for 5 to 10 minutes more or until fish flakes easily when tested with a fork. (For a gas grill, preheat grill. Reduce heat to medium. Place 1 of the fish fillets, skin side up, on grill rack over heat. Cover and grill as above.)

④ Transfer fish to a serving platter; cover and keep warm. Clean grill rack. Repeat with the remaining fish fillet.

⑤ Serve fish with relish. If desired, garnish with the thyme sprigs and serve with lime wedges.

PER SERVING 756 calories; 48 g total fat (11 g sat. fat); 187 mg cholesterol; 790 mg sodium; 7 g carbohydrate; 2 g fiber; 71 g protein

Sesame Salmon with Asian Slaw

Marinated chunks of salmon are grilled on skewers and served on a bed of ginger-seasoned coleslaw.

MAKES 6 servings **PREP** 20 minutes
MARINATE 30 minutes **GRILL** 6 minutes

———◆———

- 1½   pounds fresh or frozen skinless salmon fillets
- ⅔   cup reduced-sodium soy sauce
- ⅓   cup sesame oil (not toasted)
- ⅓   cup sherry vinegar
- 3   tablespoons grated fresh ginger
- 4   cloves garlic, minced
- ¼   teaspoon cayenne pepper
     Asian Slaw
     Sesame seeds, toasted

① Thaw fish, if frozen. Rinse fish; pat dry with paper towels. Cut fish into 1-inch pieces. Place fish in a resealable plastic bag set in a shallow dish.

② For marinade, combine soy sauce, sesame oil, vinegar, ginger, garlic, and cayenne. Pour over fish. Seal bag; turn to coat fish. Marinate in refrigerator 30 minutes, turning once.

③ Drain fish, discarding marinade. Thread fish onto twelve 4-inch wooden skewers,* leaving ¼ inch between pieces.

④ For a charcoal grill, grill fish skewers on the greased rack of an uncovered grill directly over medium coals for 6 to 8 minutes or until fish flakes easily when tested with a fork, turning once halfway through grilling. (For a gas grill, cook fish skewers over medium heat as above.)

⑤ Arrange fish skewers on top of Asian Slaw. Sprinkle with sesame seeds.

Asian Slaw: In a small screw-top jar combine 2 tablespoons vegetable oil, 1 tablespoon lime juice, 1 tablespoon rice vinegar, 1 teaspoon packed brown sugar, 1 teaspoon grated fresh ginger, 1 teaspoon soy sauce, ¼ teaspoon salt, and ¼ teaspoon crushed red pepper. Cover and shake well. In a large bowl combine 4 cups shredded cabbage, 1 cup shredded bok choy, 1 cup shredded carrots (2 medium), ½ cup thinly sliced radishes, ½ cup cucumber strips, ½ cup chopped sweet green or orange pepper (1 small), ¼ cup cilantro, and ¼ cup toasted sliced almonds. Shake dressing. Pour over cabbage mixture; toss gently to coat. Makes 6 cups.

*Tip: Soak skewers in water at least 30 minutes before using.

PER SERVING 519 calories; 38 g total fat (6 g sat. fat); 67 mg cholesterol; 1,460 mg sodium; 17 g carbohydrate; 5 g fiber; 29 g protein

Sesame Salmon with Asian Slaw

Port-Glazed Grilled Salmon with Basil-Peach Relish

When summer peaches are at their peak, pick up some to make this sophisticated entrée that combines a honey-peach relish with grilled salmon fillets slathered with port glaze.

MAKES 4 servings **PREP** 30 minutes **GRILL** 8 minutes

- 1 cup port
- 4 6-ounce fresh or frozen skinless salmon fillets, about 1 inch thick
- 2 tablespoons honey
- 2 tablespoons lemon juice
- 2 tablespoons olive oil
- 3 large ripe peaches, peeled, pitted, and chopped
- ⅓ cup snipped fresh basil
   Small fresh basil leaves (optional)

① For glaze, in a small saucepan bring port to boiling; reduce heat. Boil gently, uncovered, for 15 to 20 minutes or until reduced to ¼ cup. Set aside.

② Meanwhile, thaw fish, if frozen. Rinse fish; pat dry with paper towels.

③ For relish, in a medium bowl combine honey, lemon juice, and oil. Add peaches and the snipped basil; toss gently to combine.

④ For a charcoal grill, grill fish on the greased rack of an uncovered grill directly over medium coals for 8 to 12 minutes or until fish flakes easily when tested with a fork, turning once halfway through grilling and brushing frequently with glaze during the last 5 minutes of grilling. (For a gas grill, preheat grill. Reduce heat to medium. Place fish on greased grill rack over heat. Cover and grill as above.)

⑤ Serve fish with relish. If desired, sprinkle with the basil leaves.

PER SERVING 559 calories; 26 g total fat (5 g sat. fat); 100 mg cholesterol; 104 mg sodium; 32 g carbohydrate; 2 g fiber; 36 g protein

Marinated Tuna Steaks

A lemon and herb marinade brings enticing flavor to tuna steaks. Keep the marinating time for this zesty grilled fish to no more than 2 hours. If the tuna marinates longer, the acid in the marinade will toughen the fish.

MAKES 4 servings   **PREP** 15 minutes
MARINATE 1 to 2 hours   **GRILL** 8 minutes

- 4 6-ounce fresh or frozen tuna steaks, cut 1 inch thick
- ⅓ cup dry white wine
- 1 tablespoon lemon juice
- 1 tablespoon olive oil or vegetable oil
- 2 teaspoons snipped fresh rosemary or ½ teaspoon dried rosemary, crushed
- 1 teaspoon snipped fresh oregano or ¼ teaspoon dried oregano, crushed
- 1 clove garlic, minced
- ¼ teaspoon salt
- 4 lemon slices (optional)
- 4 fresh rosemary and/or oregano sprigs (optional)

① Thaw fish, if frozen. Rinse fish; pat dry with paper towels. Place fish in a resealable plastic bag set in a shallow dish.

② For marinade, in a small bowl combine wine, lemon juice, oil, the snipped or dried rosemary and oregano, garlic, and salt. Pour marinade over fish. Seal bag; turn to coat fish. Marinate in the refrigerator for 1 to 2 hours, turning fish once or twice. Drain fish, discarding marinade.

③ For a charcoal grill, grill fish on the greased rack of an uncovered grill directly over medium coals for 8 to 12 minutes or just until fish begins to flake easily when tested with a fork, turning once halfway through grilling. (For a gas grill, preheat grill. Reduce heat to medium. Place fish on greased grill rack over heat. Cover and grill as above.)

④ If desired, garnish fish with lemon slices and the rosemary and/or oregano sprigs.

PER SERVING 277 calories; 10 g total fat (2 g sat. fat); 71 mg cholesterol; 106 mg sodium; 0 g carbohydrate; 0 g fiber; 43 g protein

Shrimp with Sweet Pepper Relish

Leaving shells on the shrimp keeps them from burning.

MAKES 6 servings   **PREP** 25 minutes
MARINATE 2 to 4 hours   **GRILL** 3 minutes

- 2 pounds fresh or frozen medium shrimp in shells
- 1½ cups unsweetened pineapple juice
- ½ cup dark rum
- ¼ cup lime juice
- 2 tablespoons snipped fresh cilantro
- 2 cloves garlic, minced
- 1 teaspoon salt
- ½ teaspoon cracked black pepper
- 2 mangoes, seeded, peeled, and finely chopped
- ½ cup finely chopped sweet red pepper (1 small)
- ½ cup finely chopped sweet green pepper (1 small)
- ⅓ cup finely chopped red onion (1 small)
- 2 tablespoons lime juice
- 1 tablespoon red wine vinegar
- 15 whole fresh cilantro leaves
- 1 clove garlic, minced
- ¼ teaspoon salt
- ¼ teaspoon freshly ground black pepper

① Thaw shrimp, if frozen. Rinse shrimp; pat dry with paper towels. In a large bowl combine pineapple juice, rum, the ¼ cup lime juice, snipped cilantro, the 2 cloves garlic, the 1 teaspoon salt, and cracked black pepper. Add shrimp; toss to coat. Cover and marinate in the refrigerator for 2 to 4 hours.

② For relish, in a medium bowl combine mangoes, sweet peppers, red onion, the 2 tablespoons lime juice, vinegar, the cilantro leaves, the 1 clove garlic, the ¼ teaspoon salt, and the ground black pepper. Cover and chill for up to 4 hours.

③ Drain shrimp, discarding marinade. Thread shrimp onto wooden skewers,* leaving ¼ inch between pieces.

④ For a charcoal grill, grill skewers on the rack of an uncovered grill directly over medium-hot coals for 3 to 5 minutes or until shrimp are opaque, turning occasionally. (For a gas grill, cook skewers over medium heat as above.)

⑤ Spoon relish onto a platter. Arrange skewers on relish.

*Tip: Soak skewers in water at least 30 minutes before using.

PER SERVING 244 calories; 3 g total fat (1 g sat. fat); 230 mg cholesterol; 454 mg sodium; 19 g carbohydrate; 2 g fiber; 32 g protein

Spicy Chipotle Chicken Spears

Whether you're having friends come over for an after-work get-together or to watch a big game, set out a plateful of Spicy Chipotle Chicken Spears. The bacon-wrapped appetizer is undeniably a winner. Just ask Frances Blackwelder of Grand Junction, Colorado. Her zesty-tasting recipe was declared winner of the 2008 BetterRecipe.com Sports Party Food Recipe Contest.

MAKES 12 appetizer servings **PREP** 25 minutes **GRILL** 10 minutes

---

1 teaspoon onion powder
1 teaspoon garlic salt
1 teaspoon dried basil, crushed
½ teaspoon dried thyme, crushed
½ teaspoon cayenne pepper
¼ teaspoon dried sage, crushed
4 skinless, boneless chicken breast halves (about 1¼ pounds total)
12 slices bacon
1 18- to 21-ounce bottle chipotle barbecue sauce

① In a small bowl combine onion powder, garlic salt, basil, thyme, cayenne pepper, and sage.

② Cut each chicken breast half lengthwise into thirds. Sprinkle chicken with herb mixture. Wrap a slice of bacon around each chicken strip. Carefully thread each chicken strip, accordion-style, onto a 10-inch skewer.*

③ For a charcoal grill, grill chicken skewers on the rack of an uncovered grill directly over medium coals for 10 to 12 minutes or until bacon is crisp and chicken is no longer pink, turning occasionally to cook evenly and brushing with ½ cup of the barbecue sauce during the last 3 minutes of grilling. (For a gas grill, preheat grill. Reduce heat to medium. Place chicken skewers on grill rack over heat. Cover and grill as above.)

④ Serve chicken with the remaining barbecue sauce for dipping.

*Tip: If using wooden skewers, soak them in water for at least 30 minutes; drain before using.

Make-Ahead Directions: Prepare as directed through Step 2, but do not thread chicken onto skewers. Cover and chill for up to 8 hours. To serve, thread chicken strips onto skewers and grill as directed.

PER SERVING 291 calories; 18 g total fat (6 g sat. fat); 53 mg cholesterol; 903 mg sodium; 16 g carbohydrate; 0 g fiber; 15 g protein

Polynesian Honey-Pineapple Chicken

A tantalizing blend of pineapple juice, honey, and ginger acts as both marinade and brush-on for chicken drumsticks in this sure-to-please twist on grilled chicken.

MAKES 6 to 8 servings **PREP** 35 minutes **MARINATE** 6 to 24 hours **GRILL** 50 minutes

---

½   **cup unsweetened pineapple juice**
¼   **cup honey**
3   **tablespoons Worcestershire sauce**
1   **tablespoon grated fresh ginger or 1 teaspoon ground ginger**
4   **cloves garlic, minced**
1   **teaspoon salt**
12   **chicken drumsticks and/or thighs (about 3 pounds total)**

① For marinade, in a small saucepan combine pineapple juice, honey, Worcestershire sauce, ginger, garlic, and salt. Bring to boiling; reduce heat. Simmer, uncovered, about 15 minutes or until mixture is reduced to ½ cup, stirring occasionally. Cool to room temperature.

② Place chicken in a resealable plastic bag set in a deep bowl or shallow dish. Pour marinade over chicken. Seal bag; turn to coat chicken. Marinate in the refrigerator for 6 to 24 hours, turning bag occasionally. Drain chicken, reserving marinade.

③ For a charcoal grill, arrange medium-hot coals around a drip pan. Test for medium heat above pan. Place chicken on grill rack over drip pan. Cover and grill for 50 to 60 minutes or until chicken is no longer pink (180°F), brushing occasionally with the reserved marinade during the first 30 minutes of grilling. (For a gas grill, preheat grill. Reduce heat to medium. Adjust for indirect cooking. Grill as above.) Discard any remaining marinade.

PER SERVING 296 calories; 12 g total fat (3 g sat. fat); 118 mg cholesterol; 584 mg sodium; 16 g carbohydrate; 0 g fiber; 28 g protein

Southwest Grilled Chicken

Lime juice and a splash of pepper sauce lend bright, zesty flavor to grilled chicken. The recipe calls for two cut-up chickens and two pounds of chicken breasts, but any combination of parts will work.

MAKES 8 servings **PREP** 20 minutes **MARINATE** 3 to 24 hours **GRILL** 35 minutes

---

2   3- to 4-pound broiler-fryer chickens, cut up
2   pounds skinless, boneless chicken breast halves
½   cup lime juice
3   tablespoons olive oil
1   tablespoon bottled hot jalapeño sauce
2   large cloves garlic, minced
1¼ teaspoons salt
1¼ teaspoons ground cumin
    Salsa

① Place bone-in chicken pieces in a large resealable plastic bag set in a shallow dish. Place boneless chicken pieces in another large resealable plastic bag set in a shallow dish.

② For marinade, in a small bowl combine lime juice, oil, jalapeño sauce, garlic, salt, and cumin. Pour ½ cup of the marinade over bone-in chicken; pour the remaining marinade over boneless chicken. Seal each bag; turn to coat chicken. Marinate in the refrigerator for 3 to 24 hours, turning bags occasionally. Drain chicken, discarding marinade.

③ For a charcoal grill, grill the chicken on the rack of an uncovered grill directly over medium coals for 35 to 45 minutes for bone-in chicken, 12 to 15 minutes for boneless chicken, or until no longer pink (170°F for breasts; 180°F for thighs and drumsticks), turning once halfway through grilling. (For a gas grill, preheat grill. Reduce heat to medium. Place chicken on grill rack over heat. Cover and grill as above.)

④ Serve chicken with salsa.

PER SERVING 637 calories; 37 g total fat (10 g sat. fat); 239 mg cholesterol; 425 mg sodium; 2 g carbohydrate; 0 g fiber; 70 g protein

Chapter 6

HEALTHY
FAVORITES

Nutrition-rich vegetables and grains star in these low-calorie dishes.

Beef-and-Barley-Stuffed Peppers

BEEF

Beef-and-Barley-Stuffed
Peppers, 115

Teriyaki Beef and
Lettuce Wraps, 115

PORK AND LAMB

Great Greek Pitas, 116

Savory Ham
and Rice, 116

FISH AND SEAFOOD

California Wild Rice
Confetti Shrimp Salad, 119

Pasta with Seafood, 121

Scallops in
Curry Sauce, 121

Seared Salmon
with Lentils, 120

CHICKEN

Chicken and Saffron
Orzo Salad, 122

Citrus Baked Chicken, 123

MEATLESS

Black Bean and
Orange Salad, 125

Fettuccine with
Asparagus, 126

Layered Potatoes
and Leeks, 126

Veggie Chili
con Queso, 127

Teriyaki Beef and Lettuce Wraps

Beef-and-Barley-Stuffed Peppers

Try these quick-to-fix, spicy stuffed peppers for a hearty, family-pleasing meal. (Pictured on page 112.)

MAKES 6 servings **PREP** 20 minutes
BAKE 25 minutes **OVEN** 350°F

———————◆———————

3 large sweet yellow, red, and/or green peppers, halved lengthwise and seeded
1 pound lean ground beef
⅓ cup sliced green onions
1 cup cooked regular or quick-cooking barley
1 cup chunky salsa
⅓ cup shredded carrot (1 small)
¼ teaspoon ground cumin
¾ cup shredded Monterey Jack cheese (3 ounces)

① Preheat oven to 350°F. In a Dutch oven cook sweet peppers in a large amount of boiling salted water for 3 to 5 minutes or just until tender. Remove pepper halves and invert onto paper towels to drain. If desired, cover and chill for up to 24 hours.

② In a large skillet cook ground beef and green onions on medium-high heat until meat is brown, using a wooden spoon to break up meat as it cooks. Drain off fat. Stir in cooked barley, salsa, carrot, and cumin. Add ½ cup of the cheese; toss gently to combine. Spoon mixture into pepper halves. Place in an ungreased 3-quart rectangular baking dish.

③ Bake, covered, for 20 minutes. Sprinkle with the remaining ¼ cup cheese. Bake, uncovered, for 5 to 10 minutes more or until filling is heated through and cheese is melted.

PER SERVING 243 calories; 12 g total fat (6 g sat. fat); 60 mg cholesterol; 201 mg sodium; 16 g carbohydrate; 3 g fiber; 19 g protein

Teriyaki Beef and Lettuce Wraps

The lettuce provides a crisp, fresh contrast to the spicy filling.

MAKES 16 servings **START TO FINISH** 40 minutes

———————◆———————

1 large head iceberg lettuce
4 large carrots, shredded
2 cups thin sweet green pepper strips (2 medium)
6 tablespoons rice wine vinegar
½ teaspoon salt
2 pounds lean ground beef
6 tablespoons roasted garlic teriyaki liquid meat marinade
2 medium jalapeños, seeded and finely chopped*
2 tablespoons water
2 tablespoons rice wine vinegar
2 tablespoons roasted garlic teriyaki liquid meat marinade

① Remove and discard core from lettuce. Carefully remove at least 16 whole lettuce leaves; set aside. In a medium bowl combine carrots, sweet pepper, the 6 tablespoons vinegar, and salt.

② In a large bowl combine ground beef and the 6 tablespoons teriyaki marinade. Shape mixture into ½-inch meatballs.

③ Heat a very large nonstick skillet on medium-high heat. Add one-fourth of the meatballs; cook about 3 minutes or until meatballs are no longer pink, turning to brown evenly. Transfer meatballs to bowl. Repeat with remaining meatballs.

④ Return all meatballs to the skillet. Stir in jalapeños, the water, the 2 tablespoons vinegar, and the 2 tablespoons teriyaki marinade. Simmer, covered, for 3 minutes.

⑤ To serve, fill lettuce leaves with meatballs and vegetable mixture. Roll up lettuce.

*Tip: Because chiles contain volatile oils that can burn your skin and eyes, avoid direct contact with them as much as possible. When working with chiles, wear plastic or rubber gloves. If your bare hands do touch the peppers, wash your hands and nails well with soap and warm water.

PER SERVING 250 calories; 11 g total fat (4 g sat. fat); 71 mg cholesterol; 936 mg sodium; 13 g carbohydrate; 2 g fiber; 22 g protein

Savory Ham and Rice

Shorten your last-minute time in the kitchen by cutting up the vegetables and ham in advance.

MAKES 4 servings **PREP** 20 minutes
BAKE 30 minutes **OVEN** 350°F

———————◆———————

 1 cup chopped carrots (2 medium)
 ½ cup chopped onion (1 medium)
 ½ cup chopped sweet green or red pepper
    (1 small)
 ½ cup water
1½ cups cubed cooked ham (about 8 ounces)
 1 10.75-ounce can reduced-fat and reduced-
    sodium condensed cream of celery soup
 ¾ cup uncooked instant rice
 ¼ teaspoon ground sage
 ⅛ teaspoon black pepper
    Paprika (optional)

① Preheat oven to 350°F. In a medium saucepan combine carrots, onion, sweet pepper, and the water. Bring to boiling; reduce heat. Simmer, covered, for 4 to 5 minutes or until vegetables are crisp-tender. Do not drain.

② Stir ham, soup, rice, sage, and pepper into vegetable mixture. Transfer to an ungreased 1½-quart casserole. If desired, sprinkle with paprika.

③ Bake, covered, for 30 to 35 minutes or until rice is tender and mixture is heated through.

PER SERVING 227 calories; 6 g total fat (2 g sat. fat); 34 mg cholesterol; 1,028 mg sodium; 30 g carbohydrate; 2 g fiber; 12 g protein

Great Greek Pitas

Make the sauce and marinate the pork a day ahead. To serve, stir-fry the flavorful meat, spoon it into pita bread rounds, and top it with the cucumber-yogurt sauce.

MAKES 6 servings **PREP** 30 minutes
MARINATE 6 to 24 hours

———————◆———————

1¼ pounds lean boneless pork
 ¼ cup olive oil or vegetable oil
 ¼ cup lemon juice
 2 tablespoons yellow mustard
1½ teaspoons dried oregano, crushed
 1 teaspoon dried thyme, crushed
 2 cloves garlic, minced
 1 cup peeled and chopped cucumber
 1 8-ounce carton plain low-fat yogurt
 1 teaspoon dried dill
 ¼ teaspoon seasoned salt
 3 pita bread rounds, halved crosswise
    Thin red onion slices (optional)
    Thin tomato slices (optional)

① Trim fat from meat. Cut meat into thin bite-size strips. Place meat in a resealable plastic bag set in a deep bowl.

② For marinade, in a small bowl combine oil, lemon juice, mustard, oregano, thyme, and garlic. Pour marinade over meat. Seal bag; turn to coat meat. Marinate in the refrigerator for 6 to 24 hours, turning bag occasionally.

③ For sauce, in a small bowl combine cucumber, yogurt, dill, and seasoned salt. Cover and chill for up to 24 hours.

④ Drain meat, discarding marinade. Heat a large skillet on medium-high heat. Cook and stir meat, half at a time, in hot skillet about 3 minutes or until meat is slightly pink in center.

⑤ To serve, spoon meat into pita bread halves. Stir sauce; spoon on top of meat. If desired, garnish with onion and tomato.

PER SERVING 342 calories; 16 g total fat (4 g sat. fat); 54 mg cholesterol; 351 mg sodium; 22 g carbohydrate; 1 g fiber; 26 g protein

Great Greek Pitas

California Wild Rice Confetti Shrimp Salad

It's no wonder Cheri Holmgren of Joshua Tree, California, has garnered a reputation as a cook extraordinaire. As a personal chef and owner of a catering business, she has had numerous opportunities to practice to perfection. As a result, she won the grand prize at the 2010 California Wild Rice Recipe Rumble, a recipe contest for California and Nevada culinary professionals. Chef Cheri knocked out the other competitors with her truly stellar California Wild Rice Confetti Shrimp Salad.

MAKES 6 servings   **PREP** 30 minutes   **CHILL** 2 to 8 hours

- 1   pound fresh or frozen peeled and deveined cooked medium shrimp
- 3   cups cooked California wild rice, cooled
- 1   large tomato, seeded and chopped
- ¾   cup chopped sweet onion
- 3   tablespoons finely snipped fresh cilantro
- 3   tablespoons lemon juice
- 2   to 3 tablespoons seeded and finely chopped jalapeños*
- 2   tablespoons olive oil
- ½   teaspoon salt
- ¼   teaspoon freshly ground black pepper
- 1   firm-ripe avocado, seeded, peeled, and chopped
- 2   tablespoons lime juice
- 6   cups shredded lettuce
- ½   cup chopped toasted walnuts
    Lime wedges

① Thaw shrimp, if frozen. Rinse shrimp; pat dry with paper towels. Coarsely chop shrimp. In a large bowl combine shrimp, cooked rice, tomato, onion, cilantro, lemon juice, jalapeños, oil, salt, and pepper.

② In a small bowl combine avocado and lime juice; toss gently to coat. Add avocado to shrimp mixture, stirring gently to combine. Cover and chill for 2 to 8 hours.

③ Serve shrimp mixture over shredded lettuce. Sprinkle with walnuts and serve with lime wedges.

*Tip: Because chiles contain volatile oils that can burn your skin and eyes, avoid direct contact with them as much as possible. When working with chiles, wear plastic or rubber gloves. If your bare hands do touch the peppers, wash your hands and nails well with soap and warm water.

PER SERVING 326 calories; 16 g total fat (2 g sat. fat); 147 mg cholesterol; 375 mg sodium; 27 g carbohydrate; 6 g fiber; 22 g protein

Seared Salmon with Lentils

This hearty main dish makes an easy weekday meal, yet is elegant enough for a dinner party.

MAKES 4 servings **PREP** 10 minutes **COOK** 30 minutes

2	cups water
½	teaspoon salt
½	teaspoon freshly ground black pepper
1	cup brown or French lentils, rinsed and drained
4	6-ounce fresh or frozen salmon fillets
1	teaspoon salt
½	teaspoon freshly ground black pepper
½	cup finely chopped shallots (4 medium)
2	tablespoons water
¼	cup water
2	teaspoons finely shredded lemon peel
3	tablespoons lemon juice

① In a medium saucepan combine the 2 cups water, the ½ teaspoon salt, and ½ teaspoon pepper. Bring to boiling. Stir in lentils. Return to boiling; reduce heat. Simmer, covered, for 30 to 35 minutes or until lentils are tender.

② Meanwhile, rinse fish; pat dry with paper towels. Sprinkle both sides of fish with the 1 teaspoon salt and ½ teaspoon pepper. Heat a very large nonstick skillet on medium-high heat. Add fish, skin sides down; cook for 4 minutes. Turn fish; cook, covered, about 4 minutes more or until fish flakes easily when tested with a fork. Remove fish from skillet; cover loosely and keep warm.

③ Add shallots and the 2 tablespoons water to skillet. Cook on medium heat for 2 minutes. Stir in the ¼ cup water, lemon peel, and lemon juice; cook for 1 minute.

④ Divide lentils among dinner plates. Arrange fish, skin side down, on lentils. Top with shallot mixture.

PER SERVING 542 calories; 23 g total fat (5 g sat. fat); 94 mg cholesterol; 982 mg sodium; 34 g carbohydrate; 15 g fiber; 48 g protein

Pasta with Seafood

Shrimp, scallops, and clams tossed with vegetables and pasta make an unbeatable meal.

MAKES 6 servings **START TO FINISH** 35 minutes

———————◆———————

- 8 ounces peeled and deveined shrimp
- 6 ounces fresh or frozen scallops
- 12 fresh small clams
- 6 ounces dried spinach spaghetti
- 1 cup water
- 1 medium sweet yellow pepper, seeded and cut into ¾-inch pieces
- ½ cup chopped onion (1 medium)
- 2 cloves garlic, minced
- 1 teaspoon dried basil, crushed
- ½ teaspoon dried oregano, crushed
- ½ teaspoon instant chicken bouillon granules
- ¼ teaspoon black pepper
- 2 tablespoons cornstarch
- 2 tablespoons cold water
- 1 cup seeded and chopped tomatoes (2 medium)
- 2 tablespoons snipped fresh parsley
- ¼ cup grated Parmesan cheese

① Thaw shrimp and scallops, if frozen. Halve any large scallops. Rinse shrimp and scallops; pat dry with paper towels. Cover and chill until ready to use.

② Scrub clams under cold running water. In a very large bowl combine 12 cups cold water and 3 tablespoons salt. Add clams; soak for 15 minutes. Drain and rinse. Repeat 2 more times with fresh water and salt.

③ Cook spaghetti according to package directions; drain. Return spaghetti to hot pan; cover and keep warm.

④ In a large skillet combine clams, the 1 cup water, sweet pepper, onion, garlic, basil, oregano, bouillon granules, and black pepper. Bring to boiling; reduce heat. Cook about 5 minutes or until vegetables are nearly tender and clams have opened. Remove clams; discard any unopened shells.

⑤ In a small bowl combine cornstarch and 2 tablespoons water; stir into vegetable mixture. Cook and stir until thickened and bubbly. Stir in shrimp and scallops. Cook for 3 to 4 minutes or until shrimp and scallops are opaque. Stir in tomatoes and clams; heat through. Stir in parsley.

⑥ Serve seafood mixture over hot cooked spaghetti. Sprinkle each serving with cheese.

PER SERVING 239 calories; 3 g total fat (1 g sat. fat); 80 mg cholesterol; 250 mg sodium; 31 g carbohydrate; 4 g fiber; 22 g protein

Scallops in Curry Sauce

For this curry stir-fry, choose scallops that are firm, sweet smelling, and free of excess cloudy liquid.

MAKES 4 servings **START TO FINISH** 30 minutes

———————◆———————

- 12 ounces fresh or frozen sea scallops
- 1 cup cold water
- 1 tablespoon cornstarch
- 2 teaspoons soy sauce
- 1 teaspoon sugar
- 1 tablespoon vegetable oil
- 4 cloves garlic, minced
- 2 teaspoons grated fresh ginger
- 1½ cups thinly sliced celery (3 stalks)
- 1 cup thinly sliced carrots (2 medium)
- 4 ounces fresh mushrooms, quartered
- 4 green onions, cut into 1-inch pieces
- 1 teaspoon curry powder
- 2 cups hot cooked rice
- ⅓ cup chutney
   Toasted pita wedges (optional)

① Thaw scallops, if frozen. Halve any large scallops. Rinse scallops; pat dry with paper towels. Set aside.

② For sauce, in a small bowl stir together the water, cornstarch, soy sauce, and sugar. Set aside.

③ Pour oil into a wok or large skillet; heat wok on medium-high heat. (Add more oil as necessary during cooking.) Add garlic and ginger; cook and stir for 15 seconds. Add celery and carrots; cook and stir for 2 minutes. Add mushrooms and green onions; cook and stir for 1 minute. Sprinkle curry powder over vegetables. Cook and stir about 1 minute more or until vegetables are crisp-tender. Remove vegetables from wok.

④ Add scallops to wok. Cook and stir for 2 to 3 minutes or until scallops are opaque. Push scallops from center of wok. Stir sauce; add to center of wok. Cook and stir until thickened and bubbly.

⑤ Return vegetables to wok. Stir all ingredients together to coat with sauce. Cook and stir for 1 to 2 minutes or until heated through. Serve scallop mixture with hot cooked rice, chutney, and, if desired, pita wedges.

PER SERVING 305 calories; 5 g total fat (0 g sat. fat); 28 mg cholesterol; 539 mg sodium; 45 g carbohydrate; 3 g fiber; 19 g protein

Chicken and Saffron Orzo Salad

This creative salad offers an unusual mix of ricelike orzo, sweet pepper, chicken, and basil dressing.

MAKES 6 servings **PREP** 30 minutes **CHILL** 2 to 24 hours

2	cups dried orzo pasta (rosamarina)
1½	cups chopped cooked chicken (about 8 ounces)
¾	cup chopped sweet red and/or orange pepper
⅓	cup white balsamic vinegar or white wine vinegar
¼	cup olive oil
¼	cup snipped fresh basil or 1 tablespoon dried basil, crushed
¼	teaspoon salt
¼	teaspoon black pepper
	Dash ground saffron or ¼ teaspoon ground turmeric
	Fresh basil sprigs (optional)

① Cook orzo according to package directions; drain. Rinse with cold water; drain again. Transfer cooked orzo to a very large bowl. Stir in cooked chicken and sweet pepper.

② For dressing, in a small bowl whisk together vinegar, oil, the snipped or dried basil, salt, black pepper, and saffron. Pour dressing over orzo mixture; toss gently to coat.

③ Cover and chill for 2 to 24 hours. If desired, garnish salad with the basil sprigs.

PER SERVING 205 calories; 12 g total fat (2 g sat. fat); 31 mg cholesterol; 131 mg sodium; 12 g carbohydrate; 1 g fiber; 12 g protein

Citrus Baked Chicken

The orange and lemon in the marinade contribute more than just bright, zesty flavor—they also supply a welcome dose of vitamin C.

MAKES 6 servings **PREP** 20 minutes **MARINATE** 8 to 24 hours **BAKE** 40 minutes **OVEN** 425°F

- 6   bone-in chicken breast halves (about 2½ pounds total)
- 1   orange, quartered and sliced
- 1   lemon, quartered and sliced
- ¼   cup dry white wine
- 1   teaspoon snipped fresh mint or ¼ teaspoon dried mint, crushed
- 2   cloves garlic, minced
- ½   teaspoon salt
- ¼   teaspoon freshly ground black pepper
- ⅛   teaspoon ground allspice
- 1   medium onion, sliced
- ½   cup green olives, pitted

① Place chicken, orange slices, and lemon slices in a resealable plastic bag set in a shallow dish.

② For marinade, in a small bowl combine wine, mint, garlic, salt, pepper, and allspice. Pour marinade over chicken. Seal bag; turn to coat chicken, squeezing citrus slices slightly to release juice. Marinate in the refrigerator for 8 to 24 hours, turning bag occasionally. Drain chicken, reserving citrus pieces and marinade.

③ Preheat oven to 425°F. Place the onion slices in a 15 x 10 x 1-inch baking pan. Top with chicken and olives; spoon the reserved citrus pieces and marinade over the chicken mixture.

④ Bake about 40 minutes or until chicken is no longer pink (170°F).

PER SERVING 257 calories; 4 g total fat (1 g sat. fat); 110 mg cholesterol; 509 mg sodium; 7 g carbohydrate; 2 g fiber; 44 g protein

Black Bean and Orange Salad

While wintering in Fort Myers, Florida, Louise Kline entered her Black Bean and Orange Salad in the 2010 Florida Citrus Healthy, Pure and Simple Recipe Contest at the Florida State Fair. Louise, of Carrolltown, Pennsylvania, says she was thrilled when the judges liked the appealing flavor combo of sweet oranges and tangy feta cheese. She won the $500 grand prize.

MAKES 4 servings **START TO FINISH** 20 minutes

---

2   **oranges**
¼   **cup snipped fresh cilantro**
1   **tablespoon olive oil**
1   **tablespoon Dijon mustard**
2   **cloves garlic, minced**
¼   **teaspoon salt**
¼   **teaspoon ground cumin**
¼   **teaspoon black pepper**
1   **15-ounce can black beans, rinsed and drained**
¼   **cup crumbled feta cheese (1 ounce)**
¼   **cup chopped red onion**
    Lettuce leaves

① Peel and section oranges over a bowl to catch the juice. Reserve 2 tablespoons of the juice; discard any remaining juice.

② In a large bowl whisk together the 2 tablespoons orange juice, cilantro, oil, mustard, garlic, salt, cumin, and pepper. Add orange sections, beans, cheese, and red onion; toss gently to combine. Serve bean mixture over lettuce.

PER SERVING 168 calories; 6 g total fat (2 g sat. fat); 8 mg cholesterol; 612 mg sodium; 25 g carbohydrate; 7 g fiber; 9 g protein

Fettuccine with Asparagus

This Italian-inspired pasta main dish has plenty of fresh vegetables—fennel, asparagus, and tomatoes—tossed with prosciutto and Parmesan cheese.

MAKES 3 servings **START TO FINISH** 20 minutes

---

 9   ounces fresh fettuccine or tagliatelle or 6 ounces dried fettuccine or tagliatelle, broken
 1   medium fennel bulb, trimmed and cut into 1-inch pieces (1½ cups)
 1   tablespoon olive oil or vegetable oil
 8   ounces fresh asparagus, cut diagonally into 1½-inch pieces
 1½   cups peeled, seeded, and chopped tomatoes (3 medium)
 2   ounces prosciutto or cooked lean ham or turkey ham, cut into thin strips
      Salt
      Black pepper
 ¼   cup grated Parmesan cheese

① Cook pasta according to package directions; drain. Return pasta to hot pan; cover and keep warm.

② Meanwhile, in a large skillet cook fennel in hot oil on medium heat for 3 minutes, stirring occasionally. Add asparagus; cook about 4 minutes or until nearly tender, stirring occasionally. Stir in tomatoes and prosciutto; cook about 2 minutes or until heated through.

③ Add fennel mixture to cooked pasta; toss gently to combine. Season to taste with salt and pepper. Sprinkle each serving with cheese.

PER SERVING 418 calories; 13 g total fat (1 g sat. fat); 7 mg cholesterol; 480 mg sodium; 58 g carbohydrate; 3 g fiber; 19 g protein

Layered Potatoes and Leeks

This easy-on-the-cook main-dish casserole is layered with sliced potatoes, a savory leek and mushroom mixture, and Parmesan cheese. Serve it with a simple salad of mixed greens and vinaigrette dressing.

MAKES 4 servings **PREP** 25 minutes **BAKE** 35 minutes
STAND 10 minutes **OVEN** 400°F

---

 1   pound potatoes (3 medium), cut into ¼-inch slices
 1   tablespoon olive oil or vegetable oil
 3   cups sliced fresh mushrooms (8 ounces)
 ⅔   cup thinly sliced leeks (2 medium)
 2   cloves garlic, minced
 ½   teaspoon dried rosemary, crushed
 ¾   cup grated Parmesan cheese
 1   tablespoon olive oil or vegetable oil
 1   8-ounce carton plain low-fat yogurt or light sour cream

① Preheat oven to 400°F. Grease a 1½-quart soufflé dish or casserole; set aside. In a covered large saucepan cook potatoes in enough boiling, lightly salted water to cover for 3 minutes; drain. (Potatoes will not be tender.)

② Meanwhile, in a large skillet heat 1 tablespoon oil on medium heat. Add mushrooms, leeks, garlic, and rosemary; cook until leeks are tender, stirring occasionally.

③ Arrange 1 cup of the potato slices in the bottom of the prepared soufflé dish, overlapping slices if necessary. Spoon one-third of the leek mixture (about ⅔ cup) over potatoes. Sprinkle with ¼ cup of the cheese. Repeat layers 2 more times. Drizzle with 1 tablespoon oil.

④ Bake for 35 to 40 minutes or until potatoes are tender and golden brown. Let stand for 10 minutes before serving. Serve with yogurt.

PER SERVING 278 calories; 13 g total fat (4 g sat. fat); 17 mg cholesterol; 282 mg sodium; 29 g carbohydrate; 3 g fiber; 14 g protein

Veggie Chili con Queso

Satisfy your chili-loving bunch with this meatless bowl-of-red flavored with green chiles and cheese.

MAKES 8 servings **PREP** 20 minutes **COOK** 30 minutes

- 2 15-ounce cans pinto beans, undrained
- 1 28-ounce can crushed tomatoes
- 1 15.5-ounce can hominy, drained
- 1 15-ounce can red kidney beans, undrained
- 1 15-ounce can garbanzo beans (chickpeas), drained
- 1 6-ounce can tomato paste
- 1 4-ounce can diced green chiles, undrained
- 2 medium zucchini, halved lengthwise and sliced (2½ cups)
- 1 cup chopped onion (1 large)
- 1 to 2 tablespoons chili powder
- 1 teaspoon ground cumin
- ¾ teaspoon garlic powder
- ½ teaspoon sugar
-    Salt
- 1½ cups shredded Monterey Jack cheese (6 ounces)
-    Sour cream (optional)
-    Snipped fresh cilantro (optional)

① In a Dutch oven combine pinto beans, tomatoes, hominy, kidney beans, garbanzo beans, tomato paste, and green chiles. Stir in zucchini, onion, chili powder, cumin, garlic powder, and sugar. Season to taste with salt.

② Bring to boiling; reduce heat. Simmer, covered, for 30 minutes. Remove from heat. Add cheese, stirring until melted. If desired, top each serving with sour cream and garnish with cilantro.

PER SERVING 370 calories; 9 g total fat (4 g sat. fat); 19 mg cholesterol; 1,195 mg sodium; 55 g carbohydrate; 14 g fiber; 20 g protein

Chapter 7

POTLUCK
PLEASERS

Wow friends and family with these easy-to-tote, go-anywhere dishes.

Swiss Chicken Bundles

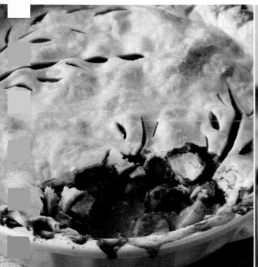  

BEEF

Aegean Casserole, 132

Deep-Dish Steak
and Vegetable Pie, 134

Go-Anywhere
Baked Beans, 131

Italian Beef and
Spinach Pie, 133

Lasagna, 130

Make-Ahead Chili-Cheese
Hoagies, 131

PORK

Salami, Fruit, and
Pasta Salad, 136

FISH

Mom's Tuna-Noodle
Casserole, 139

CHICKEN AND TURKEY

Creamy Chicken and
Spaghetti Bake, 137

Swiss Chicken
Bundles, 138

Turkey Tamale
Casserole, 139

SIDE DISHES

Broccoli-Cauliflower
Casserole, 148

Garlic-Basil Mashed
Potatoes, 149

Got-Extra-Zucchini Spoon
Bread, 143

Midwestern
Potato Salad, 146

Orzo and Bulgur Salad, 147

Spinach Pasta Salad
with Lemon Balsamic
Dressing, 141

Summer-Style Potato
Salad, 145

Triple Cheese Pasta
Casserole, 142

White Bean and Pepper
Salad, 146

Lasagna

Let the dish stand for 10 minutes before serving so the layers firm up and will hold a cut edge.

MAKES 8 servings **PREP** 45 minutes **BAKE** 30 minutes **STAND** 10 minutes **OVEN** 375°F

8	ounces lean ground beef
1	cup chopped onion (1 large)
2	cloves garlic, minced
1	16-ounce can no-salt-added tomatoes, undrained, cut up
1	6-ounce can no-salt-added tomato paste
1½	teaspoons dried basil, crushed
1½	teaspoons dried oregano, crushed
1	teaspoon fennel seeds, crushed
¼	teaspoon salt
9	dried lasagna noodles
1	12-ounce carton low-fat cottage cheese, drained
1½	cups shredded reduced-fat mozzarella cheese (6 ounces)
¼	cup grated Parmesan cheese (1 ounce)
1	egg
2	tablespoons snipped fresh parsley
¼	teaspoon black pepper

① Preheat oven to 375°F. For sauce, in a saucepan cook beef, onion, and garlic until meat is brown, using a wooden spoon to break up meat as it cooks. Drain off fat. Stir in tomatoes, tomato paste, basil, oregano, fennel seeds, and salt. Bring to boiling; reduce heat. Simmer, covered, for 15 minutes, stirring occasionally.

② Meanwhile, cook lasagna noodles according to package directions. Drain; rinse with cold water. Drain well.

③ For filling, combine cottage cheese, 1 cup of the mozzarella cheese, the Parmesan cheese, egg, parsley, and pepper.

④ Layer 3 of the cooked noodles in a 2-quart rectangular baking dish, trimming ends to fit. Spread with half of the filling. Top with one-third of the sauce. Repeat layers. Top with the remaining 3 noodles and the remaining sauce. Sprinkle with the remaining ½ cup mozzarella cheese.

⑤ Bake for 30 to 35 minutes or until heated through. Let stand for 10 minutes before serving.

PER SERVING 281 calories; 8 g total fat (5 g sat. fat); 60 mg cholesterol; 491 mg sodium; 27 g carbohydrate; 2 g fiber; 23 g protein

Go-Anywhere Baked Beans

When picnic or tailgating season rolls around, tuck this triple-bean casserole into an insulated carrier to take along.

MAKES 10 servings **PREP** 20 minutes **BAKE** 1 hour
STAND 15 minutes **OVEN** 350°F

———————— ◆ ————————

8	ounces sliced bacon
8	ounces ground beef
½	cup chopped onion (1 medium)
1	15-ounce can red kidney beans
1	15-ounce can butter beans
1	15-ounce can Great Northern beans
½	cup ketchup
½	cup packed brown sugar
¼	cup bottled barbecue sauce
2	tablespoons molasses
1	tablespoon yellow mustard
1	teaspoon chili powder
¼	teaspoon black pepper
1	cup thinly sliced smoked, cooked bratwurst (about 5 ounces)

① Preheat oven to 350°F. In a large skillet cook bacon on medium heat until crisp. Remove bacon from skillet; drain on paper towels. Crumble bacon; set aside. Discard drippings in skillet.

② Wipe out skillet. Add ground beef and onion. Cook and stir on medium heat until beef is brown and onion is tender, using a wooden spoon to break up meat as it cooks. Drain off fat. Set aside.

③ Drain kidney beans, butter beans, and Great Northern beans, reserving the liquid. In an extra-large bowl combine ketchup, brown sugar, barbecue sauce, molasses, mustard, chili powder, and pepper. Stir in bratwurst, bacon, beef mixture, and beans. Stir in enough of the reserved bean liquid to reach desired consistency.

④ Spoon mixture into a 2-quart casserole. Bake for 1 hour. Let stand for 15 minutes before serving.

PER SERVING 355 calories; 15 g total fat (5 g sat. fat); 40 mg cholesterol; 876 mg sodium; 42 g carbohydrate; 6 g fiber; 16 g protein

Make-Ahead Chili-Cheese Hoagies

For those who enjoy their sandwiches bold, serve pickled jalapeños with these crowd-pleasing hoagies.

MAKES 8 sandwiches **PREP** 35 minutes **COOL** 30 minutes
CHILL 2 to 24 hours **BAKE** 35 minutes **OVEN** 375°F

———————— ◆ ————————

1	pound lean ground beef
1	cup chopped onion (1 large)
1	cup chopped green and/or red sweet peppers (2 small)
2	cloves garlic, minced
1	14.5-ounce can diced tomatoes for chili, undrained
½	teaspoon ground cumin
¼	teaspoon black pepper
8	hoagie buns or French-style rolls
8	1-ounce slices Monterey Jack cheese or Monterey Jack cheese with jalapeños
8	1-ounce slices cheddar cheese
	Pickled jalapeños (optional)

① In a large skillet cook ground beef, onion, sweet peppers, and garlic on medium heat until meat is brown, using a wooden spoon to break up meat as it cooks. Drain off fat. Add tomatoes, cumin, and black pepper. Bring to boiling; reduce heat. Simmer, uncovered, about 15 minutes or until thick, stirring occasionally. Cool the mixture for 30 minutes or chill the mixture until ready to assemble the sandwiches.

② Split rolls lengthwise. Hollow out each roll bottom, leaving a ¼-inch-thick shell. Place a slice of Monterey Jack cheese, cut to fit, on bottom half of a roll. Spoon meat mixture on top of cheese. Place a slice of cheddar cheese on top of meat. If desired, sprinkle with pickled jalapeños. Top with roll top. Repeat with the remaining rolls, cheese, and meat mixture. Wrap each roll in parchment paper; overwrap with foil. Chill for 2 to 24 hours.

③ Preheat oven to 375°F. Place wrapped sandwiches on a baking sheet. Bake for 35 to 40 minutes or until cheese is melted and filling is hot.

PER SANDWICH 738 calories; 31 g total fat (15 g sat. fat); 91 mg cholesterol; 1,274 mg sodium; 79 g carbohydrate; 5 g fiber; 36 g protein

Aegean Casserole

The flavors of two favorite Greek specialties—moussaka and pastitsio—combine to create this new classic.

MAKES 8 servings **PREP** 1 hour **STAND** 30 minutes **BAKE** 25 minutes **OVEN** 375°F

---

4   cups milk
¼   cup butter or margarine
⅔   cup all-purpose flour
3   teaspoons salt
½   of a bay leaf
⅓   cup freshly grated Parmesan cheese
6   cups finely diced peeled eggplant
1   tablespoon olive oil
1   teaspoon olive oil
1   cup finely chopped onion (1 large)
4   cloves garlic, minced
½   teaspoon ground cinnamon
     Pinch cayenne pepper
1   pound lean ground beef
½   teaspoon dried mint
½   teaspoon freshly ground black pepper
1   28-ounce can tomatoes, undrained
¼   cup tomato paste
⅓   cup snipped fresh Italian (flat-leaf) parsley
1   16-ounce package dried ziti, cooked according to package directions

① For white sauce, in a medium saucepan heat milk over high heat until boiling. In a heavy, large saucepan melt butter over medium heat. Add flour; cook for 1 minute, whisking constantly. Gradually whisk in milk, 1 teaspoon of the salt, and the bay leaf. Bring to boiling, whisking constantly; reduce heat. Simmer and stir for 10 minutes. Remove from heat. Discard bay leaf. Stir in Parmesan cheese.

② For filling, in a large saucepan toss eggplant with another 1 teaspoon of the salt; spoon into a colander set in the sink and let stand for 30 minutes to drain. Pat eggplant dry with paper towels. In a large skillet heat the 1 tablespoon oil over medium-high heat. Add eggplant; cook and stir for 10 to 15 minutes or until tender.

③ Preheat oven to 375°F. Add the 1 teaspoon oil to skillet. Add onion; cook about 5 minutes or until tender. Stir in garlic, cinnamon, and cayenne pepper; cook for 15 seconds. Add meat, mint, the remaining 1 teaspoon salt, and the black pepper; cook until meat is brown, using a wooden spoon to break up meat as it cooks. Add tomatoes and tomato paste, breaking up tomatoes with a spoon. Add cooked eggplant. Bring to boiling; reduce heat. Simmer, uncovered, for 10 minutes. Remove from heat. Stir in parsley.

④ Transfer cooked ziti to a large bowl. Stir 1 cup of the white sauce into the ziti. Spread half of the ziti mixture in a deep 5-quart casserole. Spoon filling over; top with the remaining ziti mixture. Spoon the remaining white sauce over all. Bake for 25 to 35 minutes or until bubbly and browned.

PER SERVING 570 calories; 21 g total fat (10 g sat. fat); 67 mg cholesterol; 1,296 mg sodium; 68 g carbohydrate; 6 g fiber; 27 g protein

Italian Beef and Spinach Pie

Savory and satisfying, this cheese- and meat-filled pie is also loaded with veggies, including spinach, sweet pepper, mushrooms, and tomato.

MAKES 8 servings **PREP** 25 minutes **BAKE** 47 minutes **STAND** 10 minutes **OVEN** 450°F/350°F

1	10-ounce package frozen chopped spinach, thawed
1	unbaked 9-inch pastry shell
8	ounces lean ground beef
4	ounces mild bulk Italian turkey sausage
¾	cup chopped red and/or yellow sweet pepper
½	cup sliced fresh mushrooms
1	clove garlic, minced
1	cup water
½	cup tomato paste
1½	teaspoons dried Italian seasoning, crushed
½	teaspoon salt
¾	cup shredded mozzarella cheese (3 ounces)
⅔	cup light ricotta cheese
1	cup chopped tomatoes (2 small)
	Fresh oregano (optional)

① Preheat oven to 450°F. Drain thawed spinach well, pressing out excess liquid; set aside. Line pastry shell with a double thickness of foil. Bake for 8 minutes. Remove foil. Bake for 4 to 5 minutes more or until set and dry; remove from oven. Reduce oven temperature to 350°F.

② Meanwhile, in a large skillet cook beef, sausage, sweet pepper, mushrooms, and garlic until meat is brown and vegetables are tender, using a wooden spoon to break up meat as it cooks. Drain off fat. Stir in the water, tomato paste, Italian seasoning, and salt. Bring to boiling; reduce heat. Simmer, covered, for 10 minutes.

③ Meanwhile, in a medium bowl stir together spinach, ¼ cup of the mozzarella cheese, and the ricotta cheese. Spoon the spinach mixture into baked pastry shell. Top with the meat mixture. To prevent overbrowning, cover the edge of pastry with foil. Bake in the 350°F oven for 45 minutes. Remove foil. Top pie with tomato and the remaining ½ cup mozzarella cheese. Bake about 2 minutes more or until heated through and cheese is melted. Let stand for 10 minutes before serving. If desired, garnish with fresh oregano.

PER SERVING 290 calories; 16 g total fat (5 g sat. fat); 33 mg cholesterol; 417 mg sodium; 22 g carbohydrate; 2 g fiber; 16 g protein

Deep-Dish Steak and Vegetable Pie

Starting with refrigerated cooked beef roast is the secret to the simmered-from-scratch flavor of this homey meat pie.

MAKES 8 servings **PREP** 40 minutes **BAKE** 25 minutes **STAND** 15 minutes **OVEN** 400°F

½   of a 15-ounce package (1 crust) rolled refrigerated unbaked piecrust
¾   cup beef broth
1   teaspoon dried marjoram, crushed
2   cloves garlic, minced
¼   teaspoon salt
¼   teaspoon black pepper
2   medium parsnips (about 10 ounces), peeled and cut into ½-inch pieces
⅔   cup thinly sliced carrot
½   cup chopped onion (1 medium)
2   17-ounce packages refrigerated cooked beef roast au jus
1   cup half-and-half or light cream
¼   cup all-purpose flour
¾   cup frozen peas

① Let refrigerated piecrust stand according to package directions.

② Preheat oven to 400°F. In a large saucepan combine broth, marjoram, garlic, salt, and pepper. Bring to boiling. Stir in parsnips, carrot, and onion; reduce heat. Simmer, covered, for 10 minutes.

③ Remove meat from containers, reserving juices. Cut meat into ¾-inch pieces; set aside. In a small bowl stir together half-and-half and flour; gradually stir into vegetable mixture. Cook and stir until thickened and bubbly. Stir in meat, meat juices, and peas; heat through. Remove from heat; cover and keep warm.

④ On a lightly floured surface, roll piecrust into a circle 2 inches larger than the diameter of the top of a 10-inch deep-dish pie plate or a 2-quart casserole. Transfer meat mixture to the ungreased pie plate or casserole. Center pastry on top of meat mixture. Trim pastry 1 inch beyond edge of pie plate. Turn pastry under and flute to edge of pie plate or casserole. Cut decorative slits in pastry to allow steam to escape.

⑤ Bake for 25 to 30 minutes or until crust is golden brown. Let stand for 15 minutes before serving.

PER SERVING 387 calories; 19 g total fat (10 g sat. fat); 81 mg cholesterol; 719 mg sodium; 30 g carbohydrate; 3 g fiber; 26 g protein

Salami, Fruit, and Pasta Salad

Cantaloupe adds summer freshness to this pasta salad that has many of the great flavors of traditional Italian antipasto—artichokes, salami, and fresh mozzarella cheese.

MAKES 4 servings **START TO FINISH** 25 minutes

4	ounces dried bow tie pasta
1	12-ounce jar marinated artichoke salad (artichokes, sweet pepper, and olives) or 1½ cups deli marinated artichoke salad
1	tablespoon olive oil
1	teaspoon dried Italian seasoning, crushed
½	of a medium cantaloupe
6	ounces salami, chopped
4	ounces bocconcini (small fresh mozzarella balls), halved
	Salt
	Black pepper

① Cook pasta according to package directions. Drain and rinse under cold water; drain again.

② Drain artichoke salad, reserving ¼ cup liquid. In a small bowl combine reserved liquid, olive oil, and Italian seasoning; set aside. Peel cantaloupe. Cut cantaloupe into wedges; halve wedges.

③ In a large bowl combine cooked pasta, artichoke salad, cantaloupe, salami, and bocconchini. Pour the olive oil mixture over; toss to coat. Season to taste with salt and black pepper.

PER SERVING 448 calories; 24 g total fat (9 g sat. fat); 58 mg cholesterol; 1,057 mg sodium; 34 g carbohydrate; 3 g fiber; 22 g protein

Creamy Chicken and Spaghetti Bake

Make a complete meal by tossing a green salad and heating some dinner rolls while the cheesy chicken and pasta casserole bakes.

MAKES 4 servings **PREP** 30 minutes **BAKE** 30 minutes **OVEN** 375°F

6	ounces dried spaghetti
1	tablespoon vegetable oil
12	ounces uncooked ground chicken
1	cup sliced fresh mushrooms
¼	cup chopped onion
1	clove garlic, minced
1	tablespoon butter or margarine
1	tablespoon all-purpose flour
⅛	teaspoon black pepper
¾	cup milk
¾	cup shredded sharp American cheese (3 ounces)
¼	cup sliced pitted ripe olives
1	tablespoon snipped fresh parsley
1	tablespoon chopped pimiento
2	tablespoons fine dry bread crumbs
2	tablespoons grated Parmesan cheese
1	tablespoon butter or margarine, melted

① Preheat oven to 375°F. Grease a 2-quart square baking dish or casserole; set aside. Break spaghetti in half. Cook spaghetti according to package directions, cooking just until tender. Drain; transfer spaghetti to a large bowl.

② Meanwhile, in a large skillet heat oil on medium-high heat. Add chicken, mushrooms, onion, and garlic; cook for 3 to 4 minutes or until chicken is done, using a wooden spoon to break up meat as it cooks. Add chicken mixture to spaghetti.

③ For sauce, in a small saucepan melt 1 tablespoon butter on medium heat. Stir in flour and pepper. Add milk all at once. Cook and stir until thickened and bubbly. Cook and stir for 1 minute more. Add American cheese, stirring until melted. Remove from heat. Stir in olives, parsley, and pimiento.

④ Pour the sauce over the chicken mixture. Toss to coat. Transfer to prepared baking dish.

⑤ In a small bowl toss together bread crumbs, Parmesan cheese, and 1 tablespoon melted butter. Sprinkle over chicken mixture.

⑥ Bake, covered, for 20 minutes. Uncover; bake for 10 to 15 minutes more or until heated through.

Make-Ahead Directions: Prepare as directed through Step 4. Cover and chill for up to 24 hours. Prepare crumb mixture and chill separately. To serve, preheat oven to 375°F. Sprinkle crumb mixture over chicken mixture. Bake, covered, for 35 minutes. Uncover; bake for 10 to 15 minutes more or until heated through.

PER SERVING 516 calories; 26 g total fat (11 g sat. fat); 114 mg cholesterol; 572 mg sodium; 41 g carbohydrate; 2 g fiber; 29 g protein

Swiss Chicken Bundles

These tarragon-seasoned lasagna rolls make an elegant dish for a bridal or baby shower luncheon.

MAKES 8 servings **PREP** 40 minutes **BAKE** 30 minutes **STAND** 10 minutes **OVEN** 375°F

8	dried lasagna noodles
1	egg, beaten
2	cups ricotta cheese or cream-style cottage cheese, drained
1½	cups chopped cooked chicken or turkey
1½	teaspoons snipped fresh tarragon or basil or ¼ teaspoon dried tarragon or basil, crushed
2	tablespoons butter or margarine
2	tablespoons all-purpose flour
½	teaspoon dry mustard
¼	teaspoon salt
⅛	teaspoon black pepper
1½	cups milk
1½	cups shredded process Swiss cheese (6 ounces)
	Paprika or snipped fresh parsley (optional)
	Fresh tarragon sprigs (optional)

① Preheat oven to 375°F. Cook lasagna noodles according to package directions; drain. Rinse with cold water; drain again.

② Meanwhile, for filling, in a medium bowl stir together egg, ricotta cheese, chicken, and the snipped fresh or dried tarragon or basil.

③ To assemble bundles, spread about ⅓ cup of the filling over each lasagna noodle. Starting from a short end, roll up each noodle. Place bundles, seam sides down, in a 2-quart rectangular baking dish; set aside.

④ For sauce, in a medium saucepan melt butter. Stir in flour, mustard, salt, and pepper. Add milk all at once. Cook and stir until thickened and bubbly. Gradually add cheese, stirring until melted after each addition. Pour sauce over lasagna bundles.

⑤ Bake, covered, for 30 to 35 minutes or until heated through. Let stand for 10 minutes. Transfer lasagna bundles to 8 serving plates. Stir sauce in baking dish; spoon sauce over bundles. If desired, sprinkle with paprika or parsley and garnish with fresh tarragon sprigs.

PER SERVING 377 calories; 20 g total fat (11 g sat. fat); 111 mg cholesterol; 501 mg sodium; 23 g carbohydrate; 1 g fiber; 25 g protein

Turkey Tamale Casserole

Tamale casserole is comfort food with a Tex-Mex twist. This favorite typically features layers of ground meat, cheese, seasonings, and a cornmeal batter topper. In this simplified version, torn corn tortillas stand in for the cornmeal topper.

MAKES 6 to 8 servings **PREP** 25 minutes **BAKE** 27 minutes
STAND 5 minutes **OVEN** 350°F

- 1 pound uncooked ground turkey
- 2 cloves garlic, minced
- 1 14- to 16-ounce can cream-style corn
- 1 10.5-ounce can chili without beans
- 2 teaspoons dried oregano, crushed
- ½ teaspoon ground cumin
- ¼ teaspoon salt
- 8 6-inch corn tortillas
- 1 cup chicken broth or water
- 1 2.25-ounce can sliced pitted ripe olives, drained
- 1 cup shredded cheddar cheese (4 ounces)
  Sour cream (optional)
  Thinly sliced green onion (optional)

① Preheat oven to 350°F. In a large skillet cook turkey and garlic on medium heat until turkey is brown, using a wooden spoon to break up meat as it cooks. Drain off fat. Stir corn, chili, oregano, cumin, and salt into meat mixture in skillet. Bring to boiling; reduce heat. Simmer, covered, for 5 minutes. Remove from heat. Set aside.

② Stack tortillas; cut stack into 6 wedges. Place wedges in a medium bowl; add broth. Let stand for 1 minute. Drain, reserving ¼ cup liquid. Stir the reserved liquid and the olives into the turkey mixture. In a 2-quart rectangular baking dish layer 2 cups of the turkey mixture and half of the tortillas; repeat layers. Top with the remaining turkey mixture, spreading to cover tortillas.

③ Bake about 25 minutes or until heated through. Top with cheese; bake for 2 minutes more. Let stand for 5 minutes before serving. If desired, top with sour cream and green onion.

PER SERVING 416 calories; 21 g total fat (7 g sat. fat); 64 mg cholesterol; 988 mg sodium; 37 g carbohydrate; 2 g fiber; 24 g protein

Mom's Tuna-Noodle Casserole

If tuna noodle casserole is a dish that you remember fondly from childhood, this foolproof recipe will help you share those memories with your own family. It's hearty, satisfying, and easy to make.

MAKES 6 servings **PREP** 25 minutes
BAKE 30 minutes **OVEN** 375°F

- 4 ounces dried medium noodles
- ½ cup finely chopped onion (1 medium)
- ½ cup finely chopped celery (1 stalk)
- 2 tablespoons butter
- 1 10.75-ounce can condensed cream of mushroom soup
- ¾ cup milk
- 1 9.25-ounce can tuna, drained and flaked
- 1 cup frozen peas or peas and carrots
- ¼ cup chopped pimiento
- ¼ cup grated Parmesan cheese

① Preheat oven to 375°F. Cook noodles according to package directions. Drain and set aside.

② In a medium saucepan cook onion and celery in butter until tender. Stir in condensed soup and milk. Gently stir in tuna, peas, and pimiento. Toss tuna mixture with noodles. Spoon into a 2-quart casserole. Sprinkle with cheese. Bake for 30 to 35 minutes or until heated through.

PER SERVING 293 calories; 13 g total fat (5 g sat. fat); 39 mg cholesterol; 611 mg sodium; 24 g carbohydrate; 2 g fiber; 20 g protein

Tuna-Spinach Noodle Casserole: Prepare as directed, except substitute spinach noodles for the medium noodles, one 10.75-ounce can condensed cream of celery soup for the mushroom soup, and sliced pitted ripe olives for the pimiento. Omit Parmesan cheese. Sprinkle with snipped parsley before serving.

Tuna and Rice Casserole: Prepare as directed, except substitute 2 cups cooked rice for the noodles. Substitute one 11-ounce can condensed cheddar cheese soup for the mushroom soup and 1½ cups cooked broccoli florets for the peas.

Spinach Pasta Salad with Lemon Balsamic Dressing

How do you like your spinach? That's what Recipe4Living.com learns by sponsoring its Super Spring Spinach Recipe Contest. The 2008 winner, Joanna Gotwald of Cleveland, Ohio, answered the query with her recipe, Spinach Pasta Salad with Lemon Balsamic Dressing. This colorful whole wheat pasta salad has a rich mix of flavors and a bold, tangy dressing. Joanna serves it as a side dish with chicken, fish, or beef or as a light lunch with a generous chunk of crusty bread.

MAKES 16 servings **PREP** 35 minutes **BAKE** 35 minutes **OVEN** 400°F

½	of a head garlic
1½	teaspoons olive oil
1	teaspoon finely shredded lemon peel
¼	cup lemon juice
2	tablespoons balsamic vinegar
2	tablespoons snipped fresh basil
2	tablespoons chopped bottled roasted red sweet pepper
1	tablespoon honey
1	teaspoon sea salt
1	teaspoon coarsely ground black pepper
½	teaspoon crushed red pepper
½	teaspoon Dijon mustard
¼	cup olive oil
2	tablespoons reserved liquid from bottled roasted red sweet peppers*
8	ounces dried whole wheat penne pasta
4	cups fresh spinach leaves
1	carrot, shredded
½	of a medium cucumber, peeled, seeded, and chopped
½	of a small red onion, thinly sliced
6	ounces fresh mozzarella cheese, drained and cut into ½-inch pieces
¾	cup cherry tomatoes, halved
¼	cup chopped bottled roasted red sweet pepper

① Preheat oven to 400°F. For dressing, peel away the outer layers of the garlic bulb, leaving skins of individual cloves intact. Using a small thin knife, cut off ¼ to ½ inch of the pointed ends of the cloves, exposing individual cloves of garlic. Drizzle with the 1½ teaspoons olive oil. Wrap bulb tightly in heavy-duty foil. Bake about 35 minutes or until the cloves are soft and caramel-color. Remove from oven and unwrap until cool enough to handle. Squeeze into a cup or dish.

② In a blender combine roasted garlic, lemon peel, lemon juice, balsamic vinegar, basil, the 2 tablespoons roasted red pepper, the honey, salt, black pepper, crushed red pepper, and mustard. In a small bowl combine the ¼ cup olive oil and the reserved roasted red pepper liquid. With the blender running, slowly pour olive oil mixture through hole in lid; blend until combined. Set aside.

③ For salad, cook pasta according to package directions. Drain; cool completely. Transfer to a very large bowl. Add spinach, carrot, cucumber, onion, mozzarella, tomatoes, and the ¼ cup roasted red peppers. Pour dressing over salad; toss to coat. Serve immediately or cover and chill for up to 8 hours.

*Tip: If you prefer, substitute 2 tablespoons olive oil for the reserved liquid.

PER SERVING 148 calories; 8 g total fat (2 g sat. fat); 8 mg cholesterol; 146 mg sodium; 15 g carbohydrate; 1 g fiber; 4 g protein

Triple Cheese Pasta Casserole

Kids of all ages love mac and cheese. This recipe dresses up the old-time classic for adults. It includes sweet peppers, extra cheese, fresh oregano, and a hint of nutmeg.

MAKES 12 servings **PREP** 25 minutes **BAKE** 25 minutes **OVEN** 350°F

12	ounces dried elbow macaroni
1	16-ounce package frozen sweet pepper and onion stir-fry vegetables
3	tablespoons all-purpose flour
2	tablespoons snipped fresh oregano or basil or 1 teaspoon dried oregano or basil, crushed
¼	teaspoon salt
¼	teaspoon black pepper
¼	teaspoon ground nutmeg
3½	cups milk
8	ounces smoked Gouda cheese, shredded (2 cups)
½	of an 8-ounce package cream cheese, cut up
⅓	cup finely shredded Parmesan cheese
	Sliced roma tomatoes (optional)
	Snipped fresh oregano or basil (optional)

① Preheat oven to 350°F. Lightly grease a 3-quart rectangular baking dish; set aside. In a Dutch oven cook elbow macaroni in lightly salted boiling water for 7 minutes. Add the frozen vegetables; return to boiling. Cook about 2 minutes more or until pasta is tender. Drain well.

② In a screw-top jar combine flour, dried herb (if using), salt, black pepper, and nutmeg. Add 1 cup of the milk; shake well. Transfer to a large saucepan; add the remaining 2½ cups milk. Cook and stir on medium-high heat until slightly thickened and bubbly. Gradually add cheeses, stirring until melted. Stir in cooked pasta mixture and the 2 tablespoons snipped fresh herb (if using). Transfer to prepared baking dish.

③ Bake, covered, about 25 minutes or until heated through. If desired, garnish with tomatoes and additional fresh oregano or basil.

Tip: To tote baked casserole, wrap baking dish in several layers of newspaper and a heavy towel. Place wrapped baking dish in a large cardboard box or an insulated container to tote. Serve within 2 hours.

Make-Ahead Directions: Prepare as directed through Step 2. Cover and chill for up to 4 hours. Preheat oven to 350°F. Bake, covered, for 35 to 40 minutes or until heated through; stir. If desired, garnish as directed.

PER SERVING 202 calories; 8 g total fat (5 g sat. fat); 30 mg cholesterol; 239 mg sodium; 22 g carbohydrate; 1 g fiber; 10 g protein

Got-Extra-Zucchini Spoon Bread

Besides fresh zucchini, this colorful casserole uses other bountiful home garden treasures—corn, sweet peppers, and tomatoes.

MAKES 6 servings **PREP** 25 minutes **BAKE** 40 minutes **STAND** 5 minutes **OVEN** 350°F

1	cup fresh or frozen whole kernel corn
½	cup chopped onion (1 medium)
½	cup green sweet pepper strips (1 medium)
½	cup water
1	cup coarsely chopped zucchini
1	cup chopped tomatoes (2 small)
1	cup shredded cheddar cheese (4 ounces)
½	cup cornmeal
2	eggs
½	cup milk
½	teaspoon salt
¼	teaspoon black pepper
	Several dashes bottled hot pepper sauce

① Preheat oven to 350°F. Grease a 1½-quart casserole; set aside. In a large saucepan combine corn, onion, pepper strips, and the water. Bring to boiling; reduce heat. Simmer, covered, for 5 minutes. Do not drain. Stir in zucchini, tomato, cheese, and cornmeal. Set aside.

② In a small bowl lightly beat eggs; stir in milk, salt, black pepper, and hot pepper sauce. Stir egg mixture into the vegetable mixture in the saucepan.

③ Turn the mixture into prepared casserole. Bake about 40 minutes or until set in center. Let stand for 5 minutes before serving.

PER SERVING 198 calories; 9 g total fat (5 g sat. fat); 92 mg cholesterol; 336 mg sodium; 21 g carbohydrate; 3 g fiber; 10 g protein

Summer-Style Potato Salad

Diana Chaginian of Watertown, Massachusetts, is always looking for delicious ways to wow her husband, Alex, and daughter, Sophia, with fresh-tasting and healthful dishes. One day, Diana transformed a bag of potatoes, some tomatoes, and a few other ingredients from her pantry into Summer-Style Potato Salad. Her family not only loved it, but so did the Wisconsin Potato and Vegetable Growers Association. Diana won the 2010 Win with Wisconsin Potatoes cooking contest.

MAKES 8 to 10 servings **PREP** 35 minutes **COOK** 30 minutes

4	medium Wisconsin potatoes (such as russet)
½	cup marinated artichoke hearts, coarsely chopped
½	cup chopped green onions (4)
½	cup snipped fresh dill
2	teaspoons salt
1	teaspoon black pepper
1	tablespoon olive oil
10	to 12 fresh asparagus spears, trimmed and cut into 2-inch pieces
1	cup red and/or yellow cherry tomatoes
¾	cup olive oil or vegetable oil
2	tablespoons lemon juice
2	tablespoons Dijon mustard
2	teaspoons honey

① Add potatoes to a large pot of salted water. Bring to a simmer. Barely simmer about 30 minutes or until tender but still firm; drain. When cool enough to handle, coarsely chop potatoes and place into a large bowl.

② Add artichoke hearts, green onions, dill, 1 teaspoon of the salt, and the black pepper to potatoes in bowl.

③ In a large skillet heat the 1 tablespoon oil over medium-high heat. Add asparagus and tomatoes to hot oil; cook for 1 to 2 minutes or until tomato skins begin to burst, stirring frequently. Add asparagus mixture to artichoke heart mixture in bowl.

④ For dressing, in a screw-top jar combine the ¾ cup oil, the lemon juice, mustard, honey, and the remaining 1 teaspoon salt. Cover and shake well.

⑤ Pour dressing over salad. Very gently toss with a spoon. Serve at room temperature.

PER SERVING 263 calories; 22 g total fat (3 g sat. fat); 0 mg cholesterol; 681 mg sodium; 15 g carbohydrate; 2 g fiber; 2 g protein

Midwestern Potato Salad

Summer gatherings wouldn't be the same without a bowlful of potato salad gracing the picnic table. For a change of pace, try this version, enhanced with tender sweet corn, tangy fat-free yogurt, and fresh dill.

MAKES 10 to 12 servings **PREP** 20 minutes
COOK 12 minutes **CHILL** 3 to 24 hours

2	pounds whole tiny new potatoes or 6 medium red potatoes
1	cup thinly sliced celery (2 stalks)
¾	cup light mayonnaise or salad dressing
½	cup fat-free plain yogurt
⅓	cup chopped onion
2	to 3 tablespoons coarse-grain brown mustard or Dijon mustard
1	tablespoon snipped fresh dill or ½ teaspoon dried dill
2	teaspoons lemon juice or vinegar
½	teaspoon salt
¼	teaspoon black pepper
1	cup fresh* or frozen whole kernel corn, cooked and cooled

① Quarter new potatoes or cube red potatoes. In a large covered saucepan cook the potatoes in boiling salted water for 12 to 15 minutes or until tender. Drain and cool. Peel, if desired.

② In a large bowl combine celery, mayonnaise, yogurt, onion, mustard, dill, lemon juice, salt, and pepper. Add potatoes and corn, tossing gently to mix. Cover and chill for 3 to 24 hours before serving.

*Tip: To cook fresh corn, remove husks and silks. Rinse. Using a sharp knife, cut kernels from cob. In a small covered saucepan cook corn in a small amount of boiling water for 4 minutes; drain.

PER SERVING 177 calories; 7 g total fat (1 g sat. fat); 0 mg cholesterol; 333 mg sodium; 27 g carbohydrate; 2 g fiber; 4 g protein

White Bean and Pepper Salad

A lemon-dill vinaigrette and colorful vegetables lend garden freshness to a simple can of beans.

MAKES 6 servings **PREP** 20 minutes **CHILL** 2 to 24 hours

2	tablespoons lemon juice
1½	teaspoons olive oil or salad oil
½	teaspoon sugar
½	teaspoon snipped fresh dill or ¼ teaspoon dried dill
⅛	teaspoon black pepper
1	clove garlic, minced
1	15-ounce can cannellini beans (white kidney beans) or navy beans, rinsed and drained
½	cup chopped red or green sweet pepper
½	cup chopped, seeded cucumber
¼	cup sliced green onions (2)

① In a medium bowl stir together lemon juice, oil, sugar, dill, black pepper, and garlic.

② Add beans, sweet pepper, cucumber, and green onions. Toss to coat. Cover and chill for 2 to 24 hours before serving.

PER SERVING 57 calories; 1 g total fat (0 g sat. fat); 0 mg cholesterol; 111 mg sodium; 11 g carbohydrate; 4 g fiber; 4 g protein

Orzo and Bulgur Salad

Tired of the same old coleslaw? Try this lively salad instead. It features a delightful mix of bulgur, orzo, and fresh vegetables tossed with a balsamic vinaigrette and sweetened with a handful of dried cranberries.

MAKES 10 to 12 servings **PREP** 30 minutes **STAND** 45 minutes **CHILL** 4 to 24 hours

1	cup bulgur
1	cup dried orzo
½	cup finely chopped celery (1 stalk)
½	cup shredded carrot (1 medium)
½	cup chopped, seeded cucumber
½	cup dried cranberries
⅓	cup olive oil
¼	cup balsamic vinegar
½	cup coarsely snipped fresh parsley
2	tablespoons finely chopped shallot
1	teaspoon sugar
1	teaspoon salt
1	teaspoon dry mustard
½	teaspoon fennel seeds, crushed
¼	teaspoon black pepper
¼	cup chopped green onions (2)
¼	cup crumbled feta cheese (1 ounce)

① Place bulgur in a 2-cup glass measure; set aside. Cook orzo according to package directions. Drain orzo, reserving cooking water. Pour enough of the hot cooking water into the glass measure with the bulgur to equal 2 cups. Let bulgur stand about 45 minutes or until all of the liquid has been absorbed.

② In a large bowl combine cooked orzo, celery, carrot, cucumber, and cranberries. Add the bulgur; set aside. In a medium bowl whisk together olive oil, vinegar, parsley, shallot, sugar, salt, mustard, fennel seeds, and pepper. Add to bulgur mixture; toss well. Cover and chill for 4 to 24 hours. Stir before serving. Top with green onions and feta cheese.

PER SERVING 217 calories; 9 g total fat (2 g sat. fat); 3 mg cholesterol; 288 mg sodium; 31 g carbohydrate; 4 g fiber; 5 g protein

Broccoli-Cauliflower Casserole

This potluck pleaser features a creamy vegetable combo topped with a layer of savory stuffing.

MAKES 8 servings **PREP** 15 minutes **BAKE** 45 minutes **OVEN** 350°F

- 1   head cauliflower, cut into florets
- 1   head broccoli, cut into florets
- 2   eggs
- 1   cup coarsely chopped onion (1 large)
- 1   10.75-ounce can condensed cream of mushroom soup
- ½   cup light mayonnaise or salad dressing
- 2   cups shredded sharp cheddar cheese (4 ounces)
- 1   6-ounce package chicken-flavor stuffing mix

① Preheat oven to 350°F. In a large saucepan place cauliflower on a steamer rack over boiling water; cover and steam for 2 minutes. Add broccoli; steam for 5 to 6 minutes more or just until vegetables are tender. Set aside.

② In a food processor or blender combine eggs, onion, soup, and mayonnaise; cover and process or blend until smooth.

③ Spread cauliflower in an even layer in a 3-quart rectangular baking dish. Sprinkle with half of the cheese; spread half of the soup mixture over cheese. Repeat layering with broccoli and the remaining cheese and soup mixture.

④ Prepare stuffing mix according to package directions. Spoon stuffing over top of the layers in baking dish. Bake for 45 minutes.

PER SERVING 379 calories; 25 g total fat (11 g sat. fat); 104 mg cholesterol; 953 mg sodium; 27 g carbohydrate; 3 g fiber; 14 g protein

Garlic-Basil Mashed Potatoes

Tote these fancied-up potatoes to a potluck and get ready for rave reviews.

MAKES 10 to 12 servings **PREP** 35 minutes **BAKE** 50 minutes **OVEN** 350°F/325°F

10	cloves garlic, unpeeled
3	tablespoons olive oil
9	medium potatoes (about 3 pounds), peeled and cut up
1	8-ounce carton sour cream
¼	cup grated Parmesan cheese
¼	teaspoon salt
	Milk (about ¼ cup)
¼	cup packed fresh basil leaves, snipped
3	tablespoons grated Parmesan cheese
¼	cup butter or margarine, melted

① Preheat oven to 350°F. Grease a 2-quart casserole; set aside. Place garlic in a soufflé dish or ramekin. Drizzle with oil. Bake about 20 minutes or until garlic is very soft; cool. Peel the garlic, discarding skins and reserving oil. Reduce oven temperature to 325°F.

② Meanwhile, in a large covered saucepan cook potatoes in a large amount of boiling salted water for 20 to 25 minutes or until tender. Drain. Transfer potatoes to a large bowl. Beat potatoes with an electric mixer on low speed. Add sour cream, the ¼ cup cheese, baked garlic, reserved oil, and salt. Gradually beat in enough milk to make the mixture fluffy. Fold in basil. Spoon the potato mixture into prepared casserole.

③ Bake, covered, in the 325°F oven for 40 minutes. Stir. Sprinkle with the 3 tablespoons Parmesan cheese and drizzle with melted butter. Bake, uncovered, for 10 to 15 minutes more or until heated through.

Make-Ahead Directions: Prepare as directed through Step 2. Cover and chill for up to 24 hours. Preheat oven to 325°F. Bake, covered, for 45 minutes. Stir; sprinkle with the 3 tablespoons Parmesan cheese and drizzle with melted butter. Bake, uncovered, for 30 to 45 minutes more or until heated through.

PER SERVING 210 calories; 13 g total fat (6 g sat. fat); 22 mg cholesterol; 168 mg sodium; 20 g carbohydrate; 2 g fiber; 5 g protein

Chapter 8

HANDHELD
FAVORITES

These utensil-free sandwiches, pizzas, and wraps really shine.

Olive and Arugula Salad Pizza

TARTS, PIZZAS, AND CALZONES

Beef, Mushroom, and
Onion Tart, 152

Cheese Calzones, 155

Olive and Arugula Salad
Pizza, 153

Reuben Pizza, 154

Shrimp, Roasted Red
Pepper, and Prosciutto
Bliss, 157

Southwestern
Stuffed Pizza, 154

Upside-Down
Pizza Pies, 153

SANDWICHES

Garden Chicken
on a Bun, 160

Grilled Tuna Sandwiches
with Rémoulade, 161

Meatball Sandwiches, 158

Melon and Salami
on Rye, 159

Open-Faced Wine-Braised
Fig and Caramelized
Onion Sandwich, 163

Taverna Veggie
Sandwiches, 164

WRAPS

Cobb Salad Wraps, 165

Speedy Pesto Wraps, 164

Beef, Mushroom, and Onion Tart

A cross between pizza and a meat pie, this beef, mushroom, and onion medley can be served in big wedges as a main dish or in thin slivers as an appetizer.

MAKES 4 servings **PREP** 15 minutes **BAKE** 15 minutes **OVEN** 425°F

12	ounces lean ground beef
3	cups sliced fresh mushrooms (8 ounces)
½	of a medium red onion, cut into thin wedges
¼	teaspoon salt
¼	teaspoon black pepper
1	13.8-ounce package refrigerated pizza dough
¾	cup crumbled blue cheese (3 ounces)
	Fresh oregano sprigs and/or pizza seasoning (optional)

① Preheat oven to 425°F. In a very large skillet cook ground beef, mushrooms, and red onion on medium heat about 8 minutes or until meat is brown and onion is tender, using a wooden spoon to break up meat as it cooks. Drain off fat. Stir in salt and pepper.

② Meanwhile, grease a large baking sheet or line with parchment paper. Unroll pizza dough on the prepared baking sheet. Roll or pat dough to a 15 x 12-inch rectangle. Top dough with meat mixture, spreading to within 1½ inches of the edges. Fold edges over filling, pleating as necessary.

③ Bake about 15 minutes or until crust is golden brown. Top with cheese and, if desired, oregano and/or pizza seasoning.

PER SERVING 525 calories; 23 g total fat (10 g sat. fat); 74 mg cholesterol; 1,041 mg sodium; 49 g carbohydrate; 2 g fiber; 31 g protein

Olive and Arugula Salad Pizza

Grilled flatbread or a thin Italian bread shell spread with olive pesto serves as the base for a fresh-tasting arugula-and-olive tossed salad. (Pictured on page 150.)

MAKES 4 servings **START TO FINISH** 30 minutes

* ━━━━━━━━━━ *

2	cups baby arugula
2	to 3 tablespoons olive oil
1	teaspoon lemon juice
1	teaspoon red wine vinegar
¼	teaspoon salt
⅛	teaspoon cracked black pepper
1	16 x 10-inch Italian flatbread (focaccia) or one 12-inch thin Italian bread shell
2	teaspoons olive oil
¼	cup green or black olive pesto
6	pimiento-stuffed green olives, sliced
¼	cup shaved Parmesan cheese (1 ounce)*

① Place arugula in a medium bowl. For dressing, in a screw-top jar combine the 2 to 3 tablespoons oil, lemon juice, vinegar, salt, and pepper. Cover and shake well. Pour dressing over arugula; toss gently to coat.

② Brush both sides of flatbread with the 2 teaspoons oil. For a charcoal grill, grill flatbread on the rack of an uncovered grill directly over medium coals for 1 to 2 minutes or just until golden brown, turning once halfway through grilling. (For a gas grill, preheat grill. Reduce heat to medium. Place flatbread on grill rack over heat. Cover and grill as above.)

③ Spread flatbread evenly with olive pesto to within about 1 inch of the edges. Top with dressed arugula, sliced olives, and cheese.

*Tip: To shave the Parmesan cheese, use a vegetable peeler or a grater with large holes. The cheese needs to be room temperature otherwise, it crumbles.

PER SERVING 504 calories; 27 g total fat (4 g sat. fat); 14 mg cholesterol; 1,369 mg sodium; 51 g carbohydrate; 1 g fiber; 16 g protein

Upside-Down Pizza Pies

To create the lattice crusts, start laying strips in the middle of each dish and work your way to the edge, cutting or piecing the strips of dough to fit.

MAKES 4 servings **PREP** 20 minutes **BAKE** 25 minutes
STAND 5 minutes **OVEN** 375°F

* ━━━━━━━━━━ *

2	cups cubed cooked chicken
1	14.5-ounce can diced tomatoes with basil, garlic, and oregano, undrained
1½	cups quartered fresh mushrooms
1	8-ounce can pizza sauce
1	cup shredded pizza cheese (4 ounces)
¼	cup grated Parmesan cheese
1	11-ounce package (12) refrigerated breadsticks
	Milk
1	tablespoon grated Parmesan cheese
	Desired toppings (such as sliced green onions, snipped fresh chives, sliced pitted olives, and/ or chopped sweet pepper)

① Preheat oven to 375°F. Grease four 12- to 16-ounce individual baking dishes; set aside. In a medium bowl combine cooked chicken, tomatoes, mushrooms, and pizza sauce. Spoon mixture into the prepared baking dishes. Sprinkle with pizza cheese and the ¼ cup Parmesan cheese.

② Unroll breadstick dough. Separate along perforations to form 12 strips. Weave strips over filling to form a lattice crust on each baking dish. (Depending on the width of your dishes, you may need to cut strips to length or piece strips together.) Brush crusts with a little milk. Sprinkle with the 1 tablespoon Parmesan cheese.

③ Bake about 25 minutes or until filling is bubbly and crusts are golden brown. Let stand for 5 minutes before serving. Loosen edges and invert onto dinner plates or serve in dishes. Sprinkle with desired toppings.

PER SERVING 562 calories; 20 g total fat (8 g sat. fat); 88 mg cholesterol; 1,865 mg sodium; 52 g carbohydrate; 3 g fiber; 40 g protein

Southwestern Stuffed Pizza

Thanks to a hot roll mix, the crust is easy to make and tastes as if it's made from scratch.

MAKES 6 servings **PREP** 40 minutes
BAKE 30 minutes **OVEN** 375°F

———◆———

1½ pounds lean ground beef
1½ cups shredded cheddar cheese (6 ounces)
1 12-ounce jar salsa
1 8.75-ounce can whole kernel corn, drained
½ cup sliced pitted ripe olives
2 to 3 tablespoons snipped fresh cilantro
¾ teaspoon ground cumin
¼ teaspoon black pepper
1 16-ounce package hot roll mix
¼ cup cornmeal
½ teaspoon ground cumin
   Cornmeal (optional)
1 egg, lightly beaten
   Grated Parmesan cheese or cornmeal (optional)

① Preheat oven to 375°F. For filling, in a very large skillet cook ground beef on medium-high heat until brown, using a wooden spoon to break up meat as it cooks. Drain off fat. Stir in cheddar cheese, salsa, corn, olives, cilantro, the ¾ teaspoon cumin, and pepper. Set aside.

② Prepare hot roll mix according to package directions, except stir the ¼ cup cornmeal and the ½ teaspoon cumin into the flour mixture and increase hot tap water to 1¼ cups. Turn dough out onto a lightly floured surface. Knead about 5 minutes or until smooth and elastic. Divide dough in half. Cover and let rest for 5 minutes.

③ Meanwhile, grease an 11- to 13-inch pizza pan. If desired, sprinkle with additional cornmeal. On a lightly floured surface roll each portion of dough into a circle 1 inch larger than the pizza pan. Transfer 1 crust to pan. Top with meat mixture. Cut several slits in remaining crust. Place remaining crust on top. Pinch top and bottom edges together. Brush with egg. If desired, sprinkle with Parmesan.

④ Bake for 30 to 35 minutes or until filling is bubbly and crust is deep golden brown.

PER SERVING 551 calories; 23 g total fat (9 g sat. fat); 114 mg cholesterol; 789 mg sodium; 54 g carbohydrate; 2 g fiber; 32 g protein

Reuben Pizza

All the ingredients of the ever-popular Reuben sandwich—corned beef, sauerkraut, and Swiss cheese—top this tasty pizza.

MAKES 6 servings **PREP** 15 minutes
BAKE 30 minutes **OVEN** 375°F

———◆———

1 16-ounce loaf frozen whole wheat bread dough, thawed
½ cup bottled Thousand Island salad dressing
2 cups shredded Swiss cheese (8 ounces)
6 ounces thinly sliced cooked corned beef
1 8-ounce can (about 1 cup) sauerkraut, rinsed and well drained
½ teaspoon caraway seeds
   Dill pickle slices, chopped (optional)

① Preheat oven to 375°F. Grease a 13-inch pizza pan; set aside. On a lightly floured surface roll bread dough into a 14-inch circle. Transfer to the prepared pizza pan; build up edge slightly. Prick generously with a fork. Bake for 20 to 25 minutes or until light brown.

② Spread half of the salad dressing over hot crust. Sprinkle with 1 cup of the cheese. Top with corned beef; drizzle with the remaining salad dressing. Top with sauerkraut and the remaining 1 cup cheese. Sprinkle with caraway seeds.

③ Bake about 10 minutes more or until pizza is heated through and cheese is melted. If desired, top with dill pickle.

PER SERVING 474 calories; 23 g total fat (9 g sat. fat); 58 mg cholesterol; 1,232 mg sodium; 43 g carbohydrate; 4 g fiber; 27 g protein

Cheese Calzones

Thanks to reduced-fat products, you can indulge in these cheese-stuffed Italian turnovers without feeling guilty. Plan ahead and thaw the dough overnight in the refrigerator.

MAKES 8 servings **PREP** 35 minutes **BAKE** 20 minutes **OVEN** 375°F

Nonstick cooking spray
1 **16-ounce loaf frozen bread dough, thawed**
½ **cup chopped onion (1 medium)**
2 **cloves garlic, minced**
1 **10-ounce package frozen chopped spinach, thawed and well drained**
1 **teaspoon dried Italian seasoning, crushed**
1 **egg, lightly beaten**
1 **15-ounce carton low-fat ricotta cheese**
¾ **cup shredded reduced-fat mozzarella cheese (3 ounces)**
¼ **cup grated Parmesan cheese**
Grated Parmesan cheese (optional)
1 **8-ounce can no-salt-added tomato sauce**
½ **teaspoon dried Italian seasoning, crushed**
¼ **teaspoon garlic salt**

① Preheat oven to 375°F. Lightly coat a very large baking sheet with cooking spray; set aside. Divide bread dough into 8 pieces. Place on a floured surface. Cover and let rest until needed.

② In a covered small saucepan cook onion and garlic in a small amount of boiling water until onion is tender; drain. Stir in spinach and the 1 teaspoon Italian seasoning. In a medium bowl combine egg, ricotta cheese, mozzarella cheese, and the ¼ cup Parmesan cheese.

③ Roll each piece of dough into a 6-inch circle. Spoon 2 tablespoons of the spinach mixture onto half of each circle, spreading to within ½ inch of the edge. Top each with ¼ cup of the cheese mixture.

④ Moisten edges of dough with a little water. Fold each circle in half, pressing edges to seal. Prick tops with a fork. If desired, sprinkle with additional Parmesan cheese. Place on the prepared baking sheet. Bake for 20 to 25 minutes or until golden brown.

⑤ Meanwhile, for sauce, in a small saucepan stir together tomato sauce, the ½ teaspoon Italian seasoning, and garlic salt. Cook and stir on medium heat until heated through. Serve calzones with sauce.

PER SERVING 258 calories; 5 g total fat (2 g sat. fat); 44 mg cholesterol; 273 mg sodium; 31 g carbohydrate; 1 g fiber; 16 g protein

Shrimp, Roasted Red Pepper, and Prosciutto Bliss

The grand prize in Mama Mary's 2009 Pizza Creations Recipe contest—$5,000 and a trip to Disney World—was too big a temptation to pass up for Sheryl Reynolds of Hudson, Ohio. She knew her pizza-loving family—twin girls, Ashley and Taylor, and husband, Tom—would have a glorious time if she won. And she did—with a family standby! It was the first time Sheryl had ever entered a cooking contest. What's the secret to Shrimp, Roasted Red Pepper, and Prosciutto Bliss? Sheryl thinks it's the creamy mascarpone cheese sauce that complements the shrimp and prosciutto.

MAKES 4 to 6 servings **PREP** 30 minutes **BAKE** 8 minutes **OVEN** 450°F/425°F

---

8 ounces fresh or frozen peeled and deveined medium shrimp

1 12 x 12-inch Mama Mary's Brick Oven-Style Pizza Crust or one 12 x 8-inch Italian flatbread (focaccia)
   Nonstick olive oil cooking spray

1 tablespoon olive oil

¼ cup finely chopped shallots (2 medium)

2 ounces chopped prosciutto

4 ounces mascarpone cheese, softened

6 ounces purchased roasted red pepper pesto or Homemade Roasted Red Pepper Pesto

1 cup shredded Italian cheese blend (4 ounces)

¼ cup grated Parmigiano-Reggiano cheese

1 teaspoon dried Italian seasoning, crushed

① Preheat oven to 450°F. Thaw shrimp, if frozen. Rinse shrimp; pat dry with paper towels. Lightly coat top of pizza crust with olive oil cooking spray; set aside.

② In a large nonstick skillet heat oil on medium-high heat. Add shrimp and shallots; cook and stir until shrimp are opaque. Cool slightly. Remove shrimp and cut into ½-inch pieces. Place shrimp and shallots in a medium bowl.

③ In the skillet cook prosciutto just until it starts to crisp a bit on the edges. Remove from heat.

④ Spread mascarpone cheese evenly over crust to within ½ inch of the edges. Spoon red pepper pesto evenly over cheese. Top with shrimp and shallots, prosciutto, Italian cheese blend, Parmigiano-Reggiano cheese, and Italian seasoning.

⑤ Reduce oven temperature to 425°F. Place pizza directly on oven rack. Place a baking sheet on oven rack below pizza to catch any drippings. Bake about 8 minutes or until crust and cheese start to brown.

PER SERVING 731 calories; 46 g total fat (17 g sat. fat); 150 mg cholesterol; 1,261 mg sodium; 45 g carbohydrate; 3 g fiber; 40 g protein

Homemade Roasted Red Pepper Pesto: In a food processor combine one 12-ounce jar roasted sweet red peppers, drained; ⅓ cup grated Parmigiano-Reggiano cheese; ¼ cup packed fresh basil leaves, snipped; 2 to 3 cloves garlic, minced; and 1 teaspoon balsamic vinegar. Cover and process until nearly smooth. With the machine running, slowly add 1 cup olive oil until mixture is smooth. (Watch closely and adjust the amount as needed for desired consistency.) Season to taste with salt and black pepper. Note: This recipe makes more than you'll need for the pizza. Store extra pesto in the refrigerator or freezer. Use to toss with hot cooked pasta.

Meatball Sandwiches

For a stick-to-the-ribs meal, fill pita halves with homemade meatballs and top with fresh-tasting lettuce, tomato, and yogurt.

MAKES 4 servings **START TO FINISH** 30 minutes

1	egg, lightly beaten
¼	cup fine dry bread crumbs
¼	cup snipped fresh parsley
¼	cup fat-free milk
3	tablespoons finely chopped onion
4	teaspoons sesame seeds, toasted
1	clove garlic, minced
¼	teaspoon salt
¼	teaspoon dried mint, crushed
12	ounces lean ground beef or lamb
	Nonstick cooking spray
2	pita bread rounds, halved crosswise
½	cup shredded lettuce
½	cup chopped tomato (1 medium)
1	cup plain low-fat yogurt

① In a medium bowl combine egg, bread crumbs, parsley, milk, onion, 1 tablespoon of the sesame seeds, the garlic, salt, and mint. Add ground meat; mix well. Shape mixture into 24 meatballs.

② Coat a large skillet with cooking spray; heat skillet on medium-high heat. Add meatballs; cook until brown on all sides. Cook, covered, on low heat for 5 to 10 minutes or until done (160°F). Using a slotted spoon, remove meatballs from skillet and drain on paper towels.

③ Fill pita bread halves with meatballs. Add lettuce and tomato. Sprinkle with the remaining 1 teaspoon sesame seeds. Serve with yogurt.

Make-Ahead Directions: Prepare meatballs as directed through Step 2. Place meatballs in a shallow baking pan, cover with waxed paper, and freeze about 30 minutes or until firm. Transfer to an airtight container and freeze for up to 1 month. To use, thaw in the refrigerator overnight. Preheat oven to 350°F. Place meatballs in a shallow baking pan; add ¼ cup water. Bake, covered, about 15 minutes or until heated through. Drain. Serve as directed.

PER SERVING 380 calories; 17 g total fat (6 g sat. fat); 115 mg cholesterol; 490 mg sodium; 30 g carbohydrate; 2 g fiber; 26 g protein

Melon and Salami on Rye

The classic appetizer combo of melon and prosciutto serves as the starting point for this distinctive hero-style sandwich that also boasts salami and Jarlsberg and Gouda cheeses.

MAKES 2 servings   **PREP** 20 minutes   **CHILL** 1 to 6 hours

4   slices rye bread and/or pumpernickel bread
2   teaspoons Dijon mustard
2   to 3 ounces thinly sliced Jarlsberg cheese or Swiss cheese
2   ounces thinly sliced salami
2   ounces thinly sliced prosciutto
4   to 8 thin slices honeydew melon, peeled
2   teaspoons light sour cream
2   to 3 ounces thinly sliced Gouda cheese
2   romaine lettuce leaves, ribs removed (optional)

① Lightly spread one side of bread slices with mustard. Layer 2 of the bread slices with Jarlsberg cheese, half of the meat, and the melon. Spread a thin layer of sour cream over melon slices. Add the remaining meat, the Gouda cheese, and, if desired, lettuce. Top with the remaining 2 bread slices, mustard sides down.

② Wrap individually in plastic wrap and chill for 1 to 6 hours before serving.

PER SERVING 627 calories; 30 g total fat (14 g sat. fat); 96 mg cholesterol; 2,137 mg sodium; 56 g carbohydrate; 5 g fiber; 36 g protein

Garden Chicken on a Bun

It's okay to cheat a little. Dress up frozen chicken patties with a quick sauce made from fresh-from-the-garden tomatoes, mushrooms, kohlrabi, and garlic.

MAKES 4 servings **START TO FINISH** 35 minutes **OVEN** per package directions

4 frozen cooked breaded chicken breast patties
1 cup sliced fresh mushrooms
½ cup thinly sliced celery (1 stalk)
1 small kohlrabi, peeled and cut into thin bite-size strips
1 small onion, sliced and separated into rings
1 tablespoon olive oil
2 large ripe tomatoes, chopped
1 tablespoon snipped fresh rosemary or ¾ teaspoon dried rosemary, crushed
4 cloves garlic, minced
½ teaspoon salt
4 kaiser rolls, split and, if desired, toasted
2 tablespoons mayonnaise or salad dressing
   Lettuce leaves

① Bake chicken patties according to package directions.

② Meanwhile, in a large skillet cook mushrooms, celery, kohlrabi, and onion in hot oil on medium heat for 10 minutes, stirring occasionally. Stir in tomatoes, rosemary, garlic, and salt. Simmer, uncovered, for 5 minutes more.

③ Spread tops of rolls with mayonnaise; set aside. Line bottoms of rolls with lettuce. Add chicken patties and tomato mixture. Replace tops of rolls.

PER SERVING 538 calories; 28 g total fat (3 g sat. fat); 49 mg cholesterol; 928 mg sodium; 50 g carbohydrate; 3 g fiber; 23 g protein

Grilled Tuna Sandwiches with Rémoulade

This hearty open-face sandwich features grilled tuna steaks and a creamy rémoulade sauce. The sauce gets its crunch from giardiniera, a flavorful Italian mix of sliced marinated vegetables. You'll find it in the pickles section of most supermarkets.

MAKES 4 servings **PREP** 20 minutes **GRILL** 6 minutes

4	4- to 6-ounce fresh or frozen tuna steaks, cut about ¾ inch thick
2	tablespoons garlic- or roasted garlic-flavor oil*
	Salt
	Black pepper
½	of a 12-inch Italian flatbread (focaccia)
1	medium tomato, thinly sliced
1½	cups torn mesclun mix or mixed baby salad greens
	Giardiniera Rémoulade

① Thaw fish, if frozen. Rinse fish; pat dry with paper towels. Brush both sides of fish with oil. Sprinkle with salt and pepper. If desired, place fish in a greased grill basket.

② For a charcoal grill, grill fish on the greased rack of an uncovered grill directly over medium coals for 6 to 9 minutes or just until fish begins to flake easily when tested with a fork, turning once halfway through grilling. (For a gas grill, preheat grill. Reduce heat to medium. Place fish on greased grill rack over heat. Cover and grill as above.) Remove from grill.

③ Meanwhile, cut flatbread in half. Cut each portion in half horizontally. Add flatbread, cut sides down, to grill. Grill for 1 to 2 minutes or until light brown.

④ To assemble, line toasted sides of flatbread with tomato. Top with mesclun mix, fish, and some of the Giardiniera Rémoulade. Pass the remaining rémoulade.

Giardiniera Rémoulade: In a small bowl combine ⅓ cup drained giardiniera; ⅓ cup fat-free mayonnaise dressing or salad dressing; 3 tablespoons chopped pitted green olives; 3 cloves garlic, minced; ½ teaspoon finely shredded lemon peel; and ¼ teaspoon black pepper.

*Tip: Roasted garlic oil is a flavored olive oil that's available in specialty sections of many supermarkets. If unavailable, do not attempt to make your own flavored oil; only those prepared commercially are sure to be safe to eat. Instead, substitute 2 tablespoons olive oil and ⅛ teaspoon garlic puree or minced garlic.

PER SERVING 510 calories; 13 g total fat (3 g sat. fat); 19 mg cholesterol; 813 mg sodium; 56 g carbohydrate; 5 g fiber; 42 g protein

Open-Faced Wine-Braised Fig and Caramelized Onion Sandwich

You'll never look at figs the same way once you try Open-Faced Wine-Braised Fig and Caramelized Onion Sandwich from Ninette Holbrook of Orlando, Florida. Her vegetarian recipe won $25,000 and a culinary trip including a tour of Napa Valley in the 2009 Mezzetta America's Best Sandwich Recipe Contest. This is just one of the sensational ways Ninette loves to use fresh and dried figs. She sets off this decadent sandwich with a simple tossed green salad.

MAKES 4 servings **PREP** 25 minutes **COOK** 18 minutes **BROIL** 3 minutes

---

3	tablespoons Mezzetta Extra Virgin Italian Olive Oil
2	medium sweet yellow onions, halved and thinly sliced
1	teaspoon sugar
1	teaspoon snipped fresh thyme
½	teaspoon sea salt
½	teaspoon cracked black pepper
1	cup sliced Mezzetta Marinated Sweet Yellow and Red Roasted Peppers
3	tablespoons fig balsamic vinegar or balsamic vinegar
1	cup semisweet white wine (such as Riesling)
16	to 18 fresh or dried figs
1	cup Mezzetta Pitted Kalamata Olives
¼	cup honey
¼	cup Mezzetta Extra Virgin Italian Olive Oil
1	large loaf ciabatta bread
¼	cup butter, melted
1	cup shredded Manchego cheese (4 ounces) Snipped fresh parsley (optional)

① In a large skillet heat the 3 tablespoons oil on medium heat. Add onions, sugar, thyme, salt, and pepper. Cook, uncovered, for 18 to 20 minutes or until onions are golden brown, stirring occasionally. Stir in sweet roasted peppers and vinegar; remove from heat.

② Meanwhile, pour wine into another large skillet. Cut stem ends off figs; halve or quarter figs lengthwise. Place figs, cut sides down, in wine. Bring just to boiling; reduce heat. Simmer, uncovered, for 8 to 10 minutes or until wine is reduced to about ⅓ cup. Remove from heat.

③ Preheat broiler. Line a baking sheet with foil; set aside. In a blender combine olives, honey, and the ¼ cup oil. Cover and blend until nearly smooth.

④ Cut ciabatta loaf into 4 pieces; cut each piece in half horizontally. Brush cut sides of bread with melted butter. Arrange bread, cut sides up, on the prepared baking sheet. Broil 3 to 4 inches from the heat about 2 minutes or until bread is light brown.

⑤ Spread bread with olive mixture. Top with onion mixture, fig mixture, and cheese. Broil for 1 to 2 minutes more or until cheese is melted. If desired, sprinkle with parsley.

PER SERVING 928 calories; 47 g total fat (15 g sat. fat); 49 mg cholesterol; 1,316 mg sodium; 112 g carbohydrate; 11 g fiber; 14 g protein

Taverna Veggie Sandwiches

This Grecian-style sandwich features eggplant and tomatoes layered on bread and topped with fresh oregano and crumbled feta cheese.

MAKES 4 servings **START TO FINISH** 30 minutes **OVEN** 450°F

———————◆———————

1	large eggplant, cut lengthwise into ½-inch slices
¼	cup roasted garlic-flavor oil*
3	medium tomatoes, cut into ½-inch slices
4	large ¾-inch-thick slices sourdough, Italian, or French bread
2	tablespoons snipped fresh oregano
½	cup crumbled feta cheese (2 ounces)

① Preheat oven to 450°F. Line a baking sheet with foil; lightly grease foil. Place eggplant slices on the prepared baking sheet; brush lightly with some of the oil. Bake for 10 minutes. Add tomato slices to baking sheet; brush lightly with some of the oil. Bake about 5 minutes more or just until vegetables are tender and eggplant is light brown. Remove vegetables from baking sheet.

② Place bread slices on baking sheet. Brush one side of bread slices with some of the oil. Bake about 4 minutes or until light brown.

③ To assemble, place bread slices browned sides down. Brush unbrowned sides with the remaining oil. Top with about half of the tomato slices, all of the eggplant slices, the remaining tomato slices, and oregano. Sprinkle with cheese.

*Tip: Roasted garlic oil is a flavored olive oil that's available in specialty sections of many supermarkets. If unavailable, do not attempt to make your own flavored oil; only those prepared commercially are sure to be safe to eat. Instead, substitute ¼ cup olive oil and ⅛ teaspoon garlic puree or minced garlic.

PER SERVING 310 calories; 22 g total fat (7 g sat. fat); 28 mg cholesterol; 517 mg sodium; 23 g carbohydrate; 3 g fiber; 8 g protein

Speedy Pesto Wraps

Pesto and tomato make these quick-as-a-wink sandwiches extra flavorful.

MAKES 4 servings **START TO FINISH** 15 minutes

———————◆———————

¼	cup reduced-fat cream cheese (Neufchâtel), softened
¼	cup reduced-fat basil pesto
4	8- to 10-inch flavored, plain, or whole wheat flour tortillas or oval multigrain wraps
8	ounces deli shaved or sliced smoked turkey breast
2	cups assorted fresh sprouts (such as radish, sunflower, and/or broccoli) (optional)
½	cup chopped tomato (1 medium) or ripe avocado

① In a small bowl combine cream cheese and pesto. Spread 1 side of tortillas with pesto mixture. Divide turkey among tortillas; top with sprouts (if desired) and tomato. Roll up tortillas.

PER SERVING 288 calories; 13 g total fat (4 g sat. fat); 39 mg cholesterol; 894 mg sodium; 23 g carbohydrate; 1 g fiber; 22 g protein

Cobb Salad Wraps

These wrap-and-roll sandwiches combine all the fine flavors of Cobb salad nestled in whole wheat or Southwest-flavor tortillas.

MAKES 4 servings **START TO FINISH** 20 minutes

4 8- to 10-inch whole wheat or Southwest-flavor flour tortillas

½ cup bottled blue cheese salad dressing

4 romaine lettuce leaves, ribs removed

4 slices bacon, crisp-cooked and drained

2 green onions, cut into thin strips

2 medium roma tomatoes, seeded and cut into thin wedges

½ cup shredded mozzarella cheese (2 ounces)

8 ounces cooked chicken, shredded

① Spread one side of tortillas with salad dressing. Add lettuce, bacon, and green onions. Top with tomatoes and cheese; add chicken. Roll up tortillas.

② If desired, wrap individually in plastic wrap and chill for up to 4 hours before serving.

PER SERVING 404 calories; 26 g total fat (7 g sat. fat); 69 mg cholesterol; 734 mg sodium; 17 g carbohydrate; 10 g fiber; 26 g protein

Chapter 9

SWEET ENDINGS

Pick a perfect finish to any quick supper or special occasion.

Toasted Hazelnut Bars

BARS AND BROWNIES

Almond-Fudge
Brownies, 170

Butterscotch Shortbread
Bars, 168

Toasted Hazelnut Bars, 168

COOKIES

Chocolate-Covered
Cherry Cookies, 171

Oatmeal-Apricot
Cookies, 170

Whoopie Pie Treats, 172

PIES

Lemon Swirl Cream
Cheese Pie, 175

Rhubarb-Raspberry
Pie, 176

CAKES

Choose-a-Frosting
Cupcakes, 178

Cranberry-Black Walnut
Coffee Cake, 177

Double Chocolate-Orange
Torte, 183

FRUIT DESSERTS

Cranberry Bread
Pudding, 180

Home-Style
Apple Bake, 181

Orange Ice in
Orange Cups, 181

Triple Cherry Trifle, 182

FROZEN DESSERTS

Brown Sugar-Peach
Ice Cream, 186

Mini Ice Cream
Cookie Cups, 185

Toasted Hazelnut Bars

Toasting the hazelnuts for these rich cream cheese bars enriches their nutty flavor. (Pictured on page 166.)

MAKES 48 bars **PREP** 30 minutes
BAKE 35 minutes **OVEN** 350°F

———————◆———————

2	3-ounce packages cream cheese, softened
½	cup butter, softened
2	cups all-purpose flour
½	cup packed brown sugar
2	cups granulated sugar
1½	cups buttermilk
4	eggs
½	cup butter, melted
⅓	cup all-purpose flour
2	teaspoons vanilla
½	teaspoon salt
2	cups toasted chopped hazelnuts (filberts)
	Powdered sugar (optional)

① Preheat oven to 350°F. In a medium bowl combine cream cheese and the ½ cup softened butter. Beat with an electric mixer on medium to high until smooth. Add the 2 cups flour and brown sugar; beat until combined. Using lightly floured hands, pat mixture onto the bottom and up the sides of an ungreased 15 x 10 x 1-inch baking pan. Bake for 15 minutes.

② Meanwhile, for filling, in a large bowl combine granulated sugar, buttermilk, eggs, the ½ cup melted butter, the ⅓ cup flour, vanilla, and salt. Beat on low until combined. Stir in hazelnuts. Pour filling into crust, spreading evenly.

③ Bake about 35 minutes or until golden brown. Cool in pan on a wire rack. Cut into bars. If desired, sprinkle with powdered sugar. Store in an airtight container in the refrigerator.

PER BAR 154 calories; 9 g total fat (4 g sat. fat); 32 mg cholesterol; 78 mg sodium; 17 g carbohydrate; 1 g fiber; 2 g protein

Butterscotch Shortbread Bars

Half confection, half cookie, these sweet treats are 100 percent delicious.

MAKES 24 bars **PREP** 15 minutes
BAKE 37 minutes **OVEN** 350°F

———————◆———————

1¼	cups all-purpose flour
3	tablespoons packed brown sugar
¼	teaspoon baking powder
½	cup butter
¼	cup butter
⅓	cup granulated sugar
⅓	cup packed brown sugar
⅓	cup light-color corn syrup
1	tablespoon water
¼	teaspoon salt
½	cup coarsely chopped walnuts
½	cup coarsely chopped cashews
¼	cup whipping cream
1	teaspoon vanilla

① Preheat oven to 350°F. Line a 9 x 9 x 2-inch baking pan with foil, extending foil over edges of pan. Butter foil; set pan aside.

② In a medium bowl stir together flour, the 3 tablespoons brown sugar, and baking powder. Using a pastry blender, cut in the ½ cup butter until mixture resembles coarse crumbs. Press mixture evenly onto the bottom of the prepared baking pan. Bake about 25 minutes or until golden brown.

③ Meanwhile, in a medium heavy saucepan heat the ¼ cup butter on medium heat until melted. Stir in granulated sugar, the ⅓ cup brown sugar, corn syrup, the water, and salt. Stir in walnuts and cashews. Bring to boiling on medium-high heat, stirring constantly. Boil, uncovered, for 5 minutes, stirring frequently. Remove from heat. Stir in cream and vanilla.

④ Pour nut mixture evenly over baked layer, spreading evenly. Bake for 12 to 15 minutes more or until most of the surface is bubbly. Cool in pan on a wire rack. Using the edges of the foil, lift cookies out of pan. Cut into bars.

PER BAR 152 calories; 10 g total fat (5 g sat. fat); 19 mg cholesterol; 108 mg sodium; 16 g carbohydrate; 0 g fiber; 2 g protein

Butterscotch Shortbread Bars

Almond-Fudge Brownies

Candy-coated chocolate pieces that bake on top of the brownies eliminate the need to make frosting.

MAKES 16 brownies **PREP** 20 minutes
BAKE 30 minutes **OVEN** 350°F

	Nonstick cooking spray
½	cup all-purpose flour
½	cup ground almonds
½	teaspoon baking powder
½	cup butter
2½	ounces unsweetened chocolate, cut up
1	cup sugar
2	eggs, lightly beaten
1	egg yolk, lightly beaten
1	teaspoon vanilla
½	cup candy-coated semisweet chocolate pieces

① Preheat oven to 350°F. Coat only the bottom of a 2-quart square baking dish with cooking spray. In a medium bowl stir together flour, ground almonds, and baking powder; set aside.

② In a medium saucepan combine butter and unsweetened chocolate. Cook and stir on medium heat until melted. Stir in sugar, eggs, egg yolk, and vanilla. Beat by hand just until combined. Add to flour mixture, stirring until combined.

③ Pour batter into the prepared baking dish, spreading evenly. Sprinkle with candy-coated pieces. Bake for 30 minutes. Cool in dish on a wire rack. Cut into squares. Store in an airtight container in the freezer for up to 1 month. Thaw at room temperature before serving.

PER BROWNIE 199 calories; 12 g total fat (5 g sat. fat); 55 mg cholesterol; 112 mg sodium; 22 g carbohydrate; 1 g fiber; 3 g protein

Oatmeal-Apricot Cookies

Dried apricots brighten up this oatmeal cookie. Bake some for lunch box treats or after-school snacks.

MAKES about 36 cookies **PREP** 25 minutes
CHILL 1 hour **BAKE** 10 minutes per batch **OVEN** 375°F

1¼	cups all-purpose flour
½	teaspoon baking powder
½	teaspoon baking soda
½	teaspoon ground cinnamon
¼	teaspoon salt
¼	cup butter, softened
¼	cup shortening
½	cup granulated sugar
⅓	cup packed brown sugar
1	egg
½	teaspoon vanilla
1	cup regular rolled oats
½	cup dried apricots, finely snipped
¼	cup chopped walnuts

① In a medium bowl stir together flour, baking powder, baking soda, cinnamon, and salt. Set aside.

② In a large bowl combine butter and shortening. Beat with an electric mixer on medium to high for 30 seconds. Add granulated sugar and brown sugar. Beat until combined, scraping sides of bowl occasionally. Beat in egg and vanilla until combined. Gradually beat in flour mixture just until combined. Stir in oats, apricots, and walnuts. Cover and chill for 1 hour.

③ Preheat oven to 375°F. Shape dough into 1-inch balls. Place on an ungreased cookie sheet. Bake for 10 to 12 minutes or until edges are brown. Transfer to a wire rack; cool.

④ Store in an airtight container in the freezer for up to 1 month. Thaw at room temperature before serving.

PER COOKIE 87 calories; 4 g total fat (1 g sat. fat); 9 mg cholesterol; 51 mg sodium; 12 g carbohydrate; 1 g fiber; 2 g protein

Lemon Swirl Cream Cheese Pie

First-time contestant Kate Steward Rovner of Plano, Texas, took home $5,000, along with the Best of Show title in the Amateur Division, from the 2010 American Pie Council/Crisco National Pie Championships for her Lemon Swirl Cream Cheese Pie. Besides the Championships, the American Pie Council fosters America's love affair with pie by sponsoring National Pie Day on January 23. So mark your calendar and dish up a slice of pie!

MAKES 12 servings **PREP** 1 hour **BAKE** 30 minutes **COOL** 2 hours **CHILL** overnight **OVEN** 350°F

Lemon Curd
1½	cups crushed vanilla wafers
¾	cup finely ground toasted almonds
2	teaspoons finely shredded lemon peel
	Dash salt
7	tablespoons butter, melted
2	8-ounce packages cream cheese, softened
⅔	cup granulated sugar
2	eggs
½	cup sour cream
½	teaspoon vanilla
½	teaspoon lemon extract
½	cup whipping cream
2	tablespoons powdered sugar
½	teaspoon vanilla
	Fresh raspberries

① Prepare Lemon Curd; cool. Meanwhile, preheat oven to 350°F. For crust, in a medium bowl stir together crushed wafers, ground almonds, lemon peel, and salt. Stir in melted butter. Press mixture onto the bottom and up the side of a 9-inch deep-dish pie plate. Bake for 10 to 12 minutes or until light brown.

② For filling, in a medium bowl combine cream cheese and granulated sugar. Beat with an electric mixer on medium to high for 2 minutes. Add eggs, 1 at a time, beating on low after each addition just until combined. Beat in sour cream, ½ teaspoon vanilla, and lemon extract. Beat in half of the Lemon Curd. Pour filling into crust, spreading evenly. Spoon the remaining Lemon Curd on top of filling; swirl with a small knife to marble.

③ Bake about 30 minutes or until center is nearly set. Cool on a wire rack for 2 hours. Cover and chill overnight.

④ For whipped cream, in a small bowl combine cream, powdered sugar, and ½ teaspoon vanilla. Beat on medium until soft peaks form (tips curl). To serve, cut pie into wedges. Top each serving with whipped cream and garnish with raspberries.

Lemon Curd: In a medium saucepan whisk together ½ cup granulated sugar, 1 teaspoon finely shredded lemon peel, and ½ cup lemon juice. Whisk in 3 egg yolks, ¼ cup cut-up butter, and 2 teaspoons cornstarch. Cook on medium-high heat about 8 minutes or until mixture is thickened and comes to simmering, whisking frequently. Remove from heat. Strain through a fine-mesh sieve into a small bowl. Cover surface with plastic wrap. Cool for 30 minutes. Makes 1 cup.

PER SERVING 514 calories; 37 g total fat (19 g sat. fat); 175 mg cholesterol; 294 mg sodium; 41 g carbohydrate; 2 g fiber; 7 g protein

Rhubarb-Raspberry Pie

Apple is the hidden ingredient in this luscious double-crust rhubarb and berry pie. If you like, switch out the top crust with eye-catching pastry cutouts. Use small cookie cutters or a fluted pastry wheel to cut the rolled-out pastry into shapes. Bake the cutouts on a baking sheet and use to garnish the top of the pie before serving.

MAKES 8 servings **PREP** 30 minutes **BAKE** 45 minutes **OVEN** 375°F

Pastry for a Double-Crust Pie
- 1¾ **cups sugar**
- ⅓ **cup all-purpose flour**
- 4 **cups sliced fresh rhubarb or frozen cut rhubarb***
- 1 **cup fresh raspberries**
- 1 **medium cooking apple, peeled and coarsely shredded**

① Preheat oven to 375°F. Prepare Pastry for a Double-Crust Pie. On a lightly floured surface, use your hands to slightly flatten one portion of pastry. Roll pastry from center to edge into a 12-inch circle. Wrap pastry circle around rolling pin; unroll into a 9-inch pie plate. Ease pastry into pie plate without stretching it.

② For filling, in a large bowl stir together sugar and flour. Add rhubarb, raspberries, and apple; toss gently to coat. Transfer to pastry-lined pie plate. Trim pastry even with rim of pie plate.

③ Roll the remaining pastry into a 12-inch circle. Cut slits in pastry to allow steam to escape. Place pastry circle on top of filling; trim pastry to ½ inch beyond edge of pie plate. Fold top pastry edge under bottom pastry. Crimp edge as desired. To prevent overbrowning, cover edge of pie with foil.

④ Bake for 25 minutes. Remove foil. Bake for 20 to 25 minutes more or until filling is bubbly and top is golden brown. Cool on a wire rack.

Pastry for a Double-Crust Pie: In a large bowl stir together 2½ cups all-purpose flour and 1 teaspoon salt. Using a pastry blender, cut in ½ cup shortening and ¼ cup butter, cut up, or shortening until pieces are pea size. Sprinkle 1 tablespoon ice water over part of the flour mixture; toss gently with a fork. Push moistened pastry to side of bowl. Repeat with additional ice water, 1 tablespoon at a time (½ to ⅔ cup total), until all of the flour mixture is moistened. Gather mixture into a ball, kneading gently until it holds together. Divide pastry in half. Shape each portion into a ball.

*Tip: If using frozen rhubarb, increase the flour to ½ cup. Toss the frozen rhubarb with the flour mixture; let stand about 30 minutes or until rhubarb is partially thawed but still icy. Stir well. Gently fold in the raspberries and apple. Continue as directed, except bake pie for 50 minutes. Remove foil; bake for 10 to 20 minutes more or until filling is bubbly and top is golden brown.

PER SERVING 525 calories; 18 g total fat (7 g sat. fat); 15 mg cholesterol; 336 mg sodium; 86 g carbohydrate; 4 g fiber; 5 g protein

Cranberry-Black Walnut Coffee Cake

Whether you serve it for breakfast or dessert, this cinnamony coffee cake studded with cranberries is sure to earn you a reputation as an extraordinary baker.

MAKES 12 servings **PREP** 40 minutes **BAKE** 1 hour 15 minutes **COOL** 15 minutes **OVEN** 325°F

- 2 cups dried cranberries (8 ounces)
- 1 cup apple cider or apple juice
- ½ cup packed brown sugar
- ½ cup water
- 2 inches stick cinnamon
  Streusel Topping
- 3 cups all-purpose flour
- 1 cup granulated sugar
- 1 cup black or English walnuts, toasted and ground
- 2 teaspoons baking powder
- 1 teaspoon ground cinnamon
- ¼ teaspoon salt
- 4 eggs, lightly beaten
- 1 cup whole milk
- 1 cup butter, melted
- 1 teaspoon vanilla

① In a medium saucepan combine cranberries, apple cider, brown sugar, the water, and stick cinnamon. Bring to boiling, stirring to dissolve brown sugar. Remove from heat. Cover and let stand for 10 minutes. Drain cranberries, discarding liquid and cinnamon. Coarsely chop cranberries; set aside.

② Meanwhile, preheat oven to 325°F. Grease a 10-inch springform pan. Prepare Streusel Topping. Set aside

③ In a large bowl stir together flour, granulated sugar, ground walnuts, baking powder, ground cinnamon, and salt. In a medium bowl combine eggs, milk, melted butter, and vanilla. Add egg mixture to flour mixture; stir just until moistened. Transfer batter to the prepared springform pan, spreading evenly. Sprinkle with cranberries to within 1 inch of the edge. Sprinkle with streusel topping.

④ Bake about 1¼ hours or until a toothpick inserted near the center comes out clean. Cool in pan on a wire rack for 15 minutes. Remove side of springform pan. Serve coffee cake warm.

Streusel Topping: In a food processor combine ⅔ cup all-purpose flour, ⅓ cup packed brown sugar, ¼ cup granulated sugar, ¾ teaspoon ground cinnamon, ¼ teaspoon salt, and ¼ teaspoon vanilla. Cover and process until combined. Cut up ⅓ cup butter; add to flour mixture. Cover and process with several on-off turns until mixture resembles coarse crumbs. (Or in a medium bowl stir together flour, sugars, cinnamon, salt, and vanilla. Using a pastry blender, cut in butter until mixture resembles coarse crumbs.) Stir in ¼ cup chopped black or English walnuts.

PER SERVING 619 calories; 32 g total fat (15 g sat. fat); 132 mg cholesterol; 422 mg sodium; 77 g carbohydrate; 3 g fiber; 10 g protein

Choose-a-Frosting Cupcakes

Take your choice of vanilla, lemon, coffee, chocolate, maple, or peppermint. With this basic recipe you can make six different flavors of frosted cupcakes.

MAKES 24 cupcakes **PREP** 45 minutes **BAKE** 20 minutes **COOL** 5 minutes **OVEN** 350°F

2　cups all-purpose flour
1½　teaspoons baking powder
¼　teaspoon salt
⅔　cup butter, softened
1¼　cups granulated sugar
2　eggs
1　teaspoon vanilla
1　cup milk
　Buttercream Frosting
　Coarse multicolor decorating sugar
¼　teaspoon finely shredded lemon peel
1　teaspoon lemon juice
1　drop yellow food coloring
　Flaked coconut
½　teaspoon hot water
¼　teaspoon instant coffee crystals
　Coarsely chopped chocolate-covered coffee beans
1　tablespoon unsweetened cocoa powder
　Multicolor sprinkles
¼　teaspoon maple flavoring
　Chopped walnuts
　Demerara or turbinado sugar
4　to 6 drops peppermint extract or ½ teaspoon raspberry flavoring
1　drop red food coloring
　Crushed peppermint candies

① Preheat oven to 350°F. Grease and lightly flour twenty-four 2½-inch muffin cups or line with paper bake cups; set aside. In a medium bowl stir together flour, baking powder, and salt; set aside.

② In a large bowl beat butter with an electric mixer on medium to high for 30 seconds. Gradually add granulated sugar, beating on medium until combined. Add eggs, 1 at a time, beating well after each addition. Beat in vanilla. Alternately add flour mixture and milk, beating on low to medium after each addition just until combined. Divide batter among the prepared muffin cups.

③ Bake for 20 to 25 minutes or until a wooden toothpick inserted in centers comes out clean. Cool in pans on wire

racks for 5 minutes. Remove cupcakes from pans; cool completely on racks.

④ Divide Buttercream Frosting into 6 portions. Frost 4 of the cupcakes with the first portion of frosting; sprinkle with multicolor decorating sugar.

⑤ To the second portion of frosting, stir in lemon peel, lemon juice, and yellow food coloring, adding a little additional powdered sugar if necessary. Frost 4 of the cupcakes; sprinkle with coconut.

⑥ In a small bowl combine the hot water and coffee crystals, stirring until coffee crystals are dissolved. Stir into the third portion of frosting. Frost 4 of the cupcakes; top with chocolate-covered coffee beans.

⑦ To the fourth portion of frosting, stir in cocoa powder, adding a little additional milk if necessary. Frost 4 of the cupcakes; sprinkle with multicolor sprinkles.

⑧ To the fifth portion of frosting, stir in maple flavoring. Frost 4 of the cupcakes; sprinkle with chopped walnuts and demerara sugar.

⑨ To the sixth portion of frosting, stir in peppermint extract and red food coloring. Frost the remaining 4 cupcakes; sprinkle with peppermint candies.

Buttercream Frosting: In a very large bowl beat ¾ cup softened butter with an electric mixer on medium to high until smooth. Using 2 pounds (about 8 cups) powdered sugar total, gradually add 2 cups of the powdered sugar to butter, beating well. Gradually beat in ⅓ cup milk and 2 teaspoons vanilla. Gradually beat in the remaining powdered sugar. Beat in additional milk, if necessary, to make a frosting of spreading consistency.

Make-Ahead Directions: Prepare cupcakes as directed through Step 3. Place unfrosted cupcakes in an airtight container and freeze for up to 1 month. Thaw at room temperature before frosting. Prepare frosting as directed; cover and chill for up to 24 hours. Allow frosting to come to room temperature before using.

PER CUPCAKE 353 calories; 12 g total fat (7 g sat. fat); 48 mg cholesterol; 138 mg sodium; 59 g carbohydrate; 0 g fiber; 2 g protein

Cranberry Bread Pudding

Orange pieces and cranberries are a perfect flavor match in this old-fashioned favorite.

MAKES 12 servings **PREP** 20 minutes **BAKE** 1 hour 5 minutes **OVEN** 325°F

- 3 eggs, lightly beaten
- 2 cups whipping cream, half-and-half, or light cream
- 1⅔ cups sugar
- ¼ cup all-purpose flour
- 1 small orange
- 2 cups fresh cranberries
- ½ teaspoon almond extract
- 8 ounces rich egg bread, cut into ½-inch slices, or 8 slices firm-texture white bread

① Preheat oven to 325°F. Grease a 2-quart soufflé dish or square baking dish; set aside. In a medium bowl combine eggs, cream, 1 cup of the sugar, and the flour until smooth. Set aside.

② Using a vegetable peeler, peel off just the rind of the orange, avoiding the white pith. Reserve orange peel. Peel the remaining pith from orange; discard. Section orange.

③ In a food processor combine orange peel and orange sections. Cover and process until chopped. Add cranberries; cover and process until coarsely chopped. Transfer to a large bowl. Stir in the remaining ⅔ cup sugar and the almond extract.

④ Trim crusts from bread; discard crusts. Cut bread slices into ½-inch pieces. Add bread pieces to cranberry mixture; toss gently to combine. Pour egg mixture over bread mixture, stirring to combine. Transfer bread mixture to the prepared soufflé dish.

⑤ Bake about 65 minutes or until bread is golden brown and a knife inserted near the center comes out clean. Serve warm.

PER SERVING 331 calories; 16 g total fat (10 g sat. fat); 108 mg cholesterol; 133 mg sodium; 42 g carbohydrate; 1 g fiber; 4 g protein

Home-Style Apple Bake

All you need is a wooden spoon to mix up this cakelike dessert that's brimming with apples, raisins, and pecans.

MAKES 6 to 8 servings **PREP** 15 minutes
BAKE 50 minutes **OVEN** 325°F

———◆———

1	cup all-purpose flour
2	teaspoons baking powder
¼	teaspoon salt
2	eggs
¼	teaspoon orange extract (optional)
1	cup sugar
2	cups peeled and finely chopped baking apples (such as Rome Beauty or Granny Smith) (3 medium)
½	cup chopped pecans, toasted
2	tablespoons raisins
	Frozen whipped dessert topping, thawed (optional)
	Apple slices (optional)

① Preheat oven to 325°F. Generously butter a 9-inch pie plate; set aside. In a small bowl stir together flour, baking powder, and salt.

② In a large bowl beat eggs and, if desired, orange extract with a fork until foamy. Stir in sugar. Add flour mixture to egg mixture, stirring until combined (mixture will be stiff). Stir in the chopped apples, pecans, and raisins. Transfer batter to the prepared pie plate, spreading evenly.

③ Bake about 50 minutes or until golden brown and center appears set. Serve warm. If desired, top each serving with whipped topping and garnish with the apple slices.

PER SERVING 337 calories; 10 g total fat (2 g sat. fat); 76 mg cholesterol; 256 mg sodium; 58 g carbohydrate; 2 g fiber; 5 g protein

Orange Ice in Orange Cups

Beat the heat on a warm summer day with this refreshing citrus ice. For company, serve it in festive cups made from fresh orange halves.

MAKES 6 servings **PREP** 25 minutes **FREEZE** 8 hours

———◆———

1	orange
1	cup water
⅔	cup sugar
1½	cups orange juice
2	tablespoons lemon juice
	Orange Cups (optional)
	Fresh mint leaves (optional)

① For orange syrup, use a vegetable peeler to peel off just the rind of the orange, avoiding the white pith.

② In a small saucepan combine orange peel, the water, and sugar. Bring to boiling, stirring until sugar is dissolved; reduce heat. Simmer, covered, for 5 minutes. Strain through a fine-mesh sieve into a medium bowl; discard peel. Cool orange syrup.

③ Stir orange juice and lemon juice into orange syrup. Pour mixture into an 8 x 4 x 2-inch loaf pan. Cover and freeze about 8 hours or until firm.

④ To serve, break frozen mixture into chunks; place in a metal bowl. Beat with an electric mixer on low just until slushy. If desired, serve in Orange Cups and garnish with mint.

PER SERVING 126 calories; 0 g total fat; 0 mg cholesterol; 2 mg sodium; 32 g carbohydrate; 1 g fiber; 1 g protein

Orange Cups: Cut 3 oranges into halves. Scoop out pulp with a grapefruit knife or a spoon and save for another time. Using a knife or scissors, cut a saw-toothed or scalloped edge around each orange half.

Triple Cherry Trifle

Red and yellow sweet cherries star in this dessert favorite with layers of custard, almonds, and pound cake. It's topped with billows of whipped cream.

MAKES 8 servings **PREP** 35 minutes **CHILL** 5 to 24 hours

- 3 eggs, lightly beaten
- 2 cups milk, half-and-half, or light cream
- ¼ cup sugar
- 1 teaspoon vanilla
- 1 10.75-ounce loaf frozen pound cake, thawed
- ¼ cup cherry preserves
- 3 tablespoons cherry liqueur or unsweetened cherry or orange juice
- 2 cups halved and pitted fresh dark and/or light sweet cherries
- 2 tablespoons toasted sliced almonds
- ½ cup whipping cream
- 1 tablespoon sugar
- ½ teaspoon vanilla
- Fresh mint sprig (optional)

① For custard, in a medium heavy saucepan combine eggs, milk, and the ¼ cup sugar. Cook and stir on medium heat just until mixture coats a metal spoon. Remove from heat. Stir in the 1 teaspoon vanilla. Quickly cool by placing the saucepan in a sink or bowl of ice water for 1 to 2 minutes, stirring constantly. Cover surface with plastic wrap; chill for 2 hours.

② Cut cake into ½-inch cubes (you should have about 5 cups).

③ In a 1½-quart bowl or 8 dessert dishes layer half of the preserves, half of the cake, and half of the liqueur. Dot with the remaining preserves. Top with half of the cherries, half of the almonds, and half of the custard. Repeat layers without preserves. Cover and chill for 3 to 24 hours.

④ For whipped cream, in a small bowl combine whipping cream, the 1 tablespoon sugar, and the ½ teaspoon vanilla. Beat with an electric mixer on medium until soft peaks form (tips curl). Spoon whipped cream on top of trifle. If desired, garnish with mint.

PER SERVING 361 calories; 18 g total fat (6 g sat. fat); 105 mg cholesterol; 175 mg sodium; 43 g carbohydrate; 1 g fiber; 7 g protein

Double Chocolate-Orange Torte

Unsweetened chocolate in the cake and semisweet chocolate in the icing make this orange-flavored torte extra rich and delicious. You can frost the cake several hours before serving.

MAKES 12 servings **PREP** 45 minutes **BAKE** 35 minutes **COOL** 10 minutes **OVEN** 350°F

---

3 ounces unsweetened chocolate, coarsely chopped
¾ cup all-purpose flour
1½ teaspoons baking powder
½ teaspoon baking soda
½ teaspoon salt
½ cup butter, softened
1 cup sugar
4 eggs
2 tablespoons orange liqueur or orange juice
½ cup water
1 tablespoon finely shredded orange peel
⅓ cup whipping cream
1 tablespoon light-color corn syrup
6 ounces semisweet chocolate, finely chopped, or 1 cup semisweet chocolate pieces
1 tablespoon orange liqueur or orange juice
1 tablespoon orange juice
½ cup orange marmalade
Kumquat slices (optional)

① Preheat oven to 350°F. Grease and flour an 8 x 8 x 2-inch baking pan; set aside.

② In a small saucepan cook and stir unsweetened chocolate on low heat until melted; cool. In a small bowl stir together flour, baking powder, baking soda, and salt; set aside.

③ In a large bowl beat butter with an electric mixer on medium to high for 30 seconds. Gradually add sugar, beating on medium until combined. Add eggs, 1 at a time, beating well after each addition. Beat in melted chocolate and the 2 tablespoons liqueur. Alternately add flour mixture and the water to egg mixture, beating on low after each addition just until combined. Stir in orange peel. Pour batter into the prepared baking pan, spreading evenly.

④ Bake about 35 minutes or until a toothpick inserted near center comes out clean. Cool in pan on a wire rack for 10 minutes. Loosen edges of cake; invert onto wire rack. Cool completely.

⑤ For icing, in a small heavy saucepan combine cream and corn syrup. Bring just to boiling, stirring constantly. Remove from heat. Stir in semisweet chocolate until mixture is smooth. Cool to room temperature. Stir before using.

⑥ In a small bowl combine the 1 tablespoon liqueur and orange juice. Split cake in half horizontally. Sprinkle cut sides of cake with liqueur mixture. Place bottom of cake, cut side up, on a platter; spread with marmalade. Add top of cake, cut side down. Frost cake with icing. If desired, garnish with kumquat slices.

PER SERVING 364 calories; 21 g total fat (12 g sat. fat); 102 mg cholesterol; 316 mg sodium; 43 g carbohydrate; 3 g fiber; 5 g protein

Mini Ice Cream Cookie Cups

Sue Compton of Delanco, New Jersey, loves having her son, Jon, and his friends show up so she can feed them. On a whim, Sue used several of her young crowd's favorite flavors in Mini Ice Cream Cookie Cups and entered the recipe in the prestigious 44th Annual Pillsbury Bake-Off. This was Sue's first-ever contest, and no one was more astonished than she when her easy-yet-elegant dessert won the $1 million grand prize and national television coverage, including an appearance on The Oprah Winfrey Show.

MAKES 24 cookie cups **PREP** 25 minutes **BAKE** 15 minutes **FREEZE** 5 minutes **OVEN** 350°F

Nonstick cooking spray
1 **16-ounce package (24 cookies) Pillsbury Ready to Bake! Sugar Cookies**
4 **teaspoons sugar**
⅓ **cup Fischer Chef's Naturals Chopped Walnuts**
½ **cup semisweet chocolate pieces**
¼ **cup Smuckers Seedless Red Raspberry Jam**
1½ **cups vanilla bean ice cream**
24 **fresh raspberries**

① Preheat oven to 350°F. Lightly coat twenty-four 1¾-inch muffin cups with cooking spray. Place cookie dough rounds in muffin cups. Bake for 15 to 20 minutes or until golden brown.

② Place 2 teaspoons of the sugar in a small bowl. Dip the end of a wooden spoon handle into sugar; carefully press into center of each cookie to make a 1-inch-wide indentation. Cool completely in pan.

③ Meanwhile, in a small bowl combine walnuts and the remaining 2 teaspoons sugar; set aside. In a small microwave-safe bowl microwave chocolate on high for 30 to 60 seconds or until melted and smooth, stirring once halfway through cooking.

④ Loosen edges of cookie cups; gently remove from pan. Dip rim of each cookie cup into melted chocolate, then into walnut mixture. Place in a 15 x 10 x 1-inch baking pan.

⑤ In another small microwave-safe bowl microwave jam on high about 15 seconds or until melted. Spoon ½ teaspoon of the jam into each cookie cup. Let stand in freezer about 5 minutes or until chocolate is set.

⑥ Using a small cookie scoop or measuring spoon, spoon ice cream onto cups. Top with raspberries. Store in the freezer for up to 1 week. Let stand at room temperature for 5 minutes before serving.

PER COOKIE CUP 142 calories; 7 g total fat (2 g sat. fat); 9 mg cholesterol; 88 mg sodium; 19 g carbohydrate; 1 g fiber; 2 g protein

Brown Sugar-Peach Ice Cream

Fresh peaches are best, but if you like, you can substitute one thawed 16-ounce package frozen unsweetened peach slices for the fresh.

MAKES 16 servings **PREP** 25 minutes **FREEZE** per manufacturer's directions

1½ cups milk
3 eggs, lightly beaten
1½ cups whipping cream
1 teaspoon vanilla
¾ cup packed brown sugar
3 cups peeled and finely chopped peaches (4 medium)
½ cup packed brown sugar
1 tablespoon lemon juice

① In a large heavy saucepan heat milk on medium heat just until it starts to bubble around the edge. Gradually stir milk into beaten eggs. Return to saucepan. Cook and stir on medium heat about 2 minutes or until heated through. Remove from heat; cool slightly. Stir in cream and vanilla. Add the ¾ cup brown sugar, stirring until dissolved. Cover and chill.

② In a medium bowl combine peaches, the ½ cup brown sugar, and lemon juice. Stir peach mixture into chilled cream mixture.

③ Freeze peach mixture in a 4- or 5-quart ice cream freezer according to the manufacturer's directions. If desired, ripen for at least 4 hours.

PER SERVING 180 calories; 10 g total fat (6 g sat. fat); 72 mg cholesterol; 36 mg sodium; 22 g carbohydrate; 0 g fiber; 3 g protein

Index

Note: Page references in **bold** type indicate photographs.

A
Aegean Casserole, 132
Almonds
    Almond-Fudge Brownies, 170
    Toasted Almonds with Rosemary
      and Cayenne, 27, **27**
Apple Bake, Home-Style, 181
Apricot-Oatmeal Cookies, 170
Artichoke Hearts, Potatoes, and Capers,
    Eggs in Purgatory with, **34,** 35
Arugula and Olive Salad Pizza, **150,** 153
Arugula Pesto Dip, 8
Asian Slaw, 104
Asparagus, Fettuccine with, 126

B
Bacon and Gorgonzola Cornbread
    Sliders with Chipotle Mayo, **16,** 17
Balsamic Pork Chops, 61
Barley-and-Beef-Stuffed Peppers, **112,** 115
Beans and lentils
    Black Bean and Orange Salad, **124,** 125
    Chunky Vegetable Chili, 75
    Go-Anywhere Baked Beans, 131
    Pasta with Chicken, Green Beans,
      and Hazelnuts, 66, **66**
    Pasta with Lentil Sauce, 89
    Seared Salmon with Lentils, 120, **120**
    Tuscan Ham and Bean Soup, 80, **80**
    Veggie Chili con Queso, 127, **127**
    White Bean and Pepper Salad, 146
Beef. *See also* Bison
    Aegean Casserole, 132
    Bacon and Gorgonzola Cornbread
      Sliders with Chipotle Mayo, **16,** 17
    Beef, Mushroom, and Onion Tart,
      152, **152**
    Beef-and-Barley-Stuffed Peppers,
      112, 115
    Cajun Pot Roast, **72,** 74
    Caprese Pasta and Steak, 52, **53**
    Corned Beef Hash Patties, 58

Country Swiss Steak, 75
Cranberry-Pistachio Pâté, 12, **13**
Deep-Dish Steak and Vegetable
    Pie, 134, **135**
Flank Steak with Parsley and
    Lemon, 58
Gingered Beef Stir-Fry, **50,** 52
Go-Anywhere Baked Beans, 131
Grilled Flank Steak and Onions, 96
Grilled Steak and Plum Pizzettes, **54,** 55
Herb Cheese-Stuffed Steaks, 97, **97**
Italian Beef and Spinach Pie, 133
Lasagna, 130, **130**
Make-Ahead Chili-Cheese Hoagies, 131
Meatball Sandwiches, 158
Mexican Meatballs, 22, **23**
Reuben Pizza, 154
Sizzling Steak and Peaches, 94, **94**
Skirt Steak Fajitas with Grilled
    Onions and Peppers, 95, **95**
Smothered Steak with Honeyed Red
    Onion, 56, **56**
Southwestern Stuffed Pizza, 154
Spinach and Basil Salad with Beef,
    57, **57**
Stay-Awake Steak, 96
Teriyaki Beef and Lettuce Wraps,
    114, 115
Tri-Tip Steaks with Texas Toast, 98, **98**
Bison Burgers, Smoky Barbecued, 99, **99**
Bite-Size Chicken Enchiladas, 18, **18**
Black Bean and Orange Salad, **124,** 125
Blueberry Breakfast Scones, 45
Blue Cheese Ball, 14
Bourbon-Molasses-Glazed Chicken
    Wings, 20, **21**
Brats with Mango Relish, 100, **101**
Bread Pudding, Cranberry, 180, **180**
Breads. *See also* Muffins; Scones
    Breakfast Popovers, 47
    Giant Cinnamon Rolls, 43
    No-Fry French Toast, 37, **37**
    Orange Sticky Rolls, 40, **40**
    Pecan-Praline Cinnamon Rolls, **42,** 43
Breakfast Popovers, 47
Brie-Pecan Quesadillas, 20
Broccoli and Ginger, Pasta with, 70

Broccoli-Cauliflower Casserole, 148, **148**
Brownies, Almond-Fudge, 170
Brown Sugar-Peach Ice Cream, 186, **186**
Bulgur and Orzo Salad, 147, **147**
Burgers
    Bacon and Gorgonzola Cornbread
      Sliders with Chipotle Mayo, **16,** 17
    Mediterranean Burgers, **92,** 100
    Smoky Barbecued Bison Burgers,
      99, **99**
Buttercream Frosting, 178
Butterscotch Shortbread Bars, 168, **169**

C
Cabbage. *See also* Sauerkraut
    Sesame Salmon with Asian Slaw,
      104, **105**
Cajun Pot Roast, **72,** 74
Cakes
    Choose-a-Frosting Cupcakes, 178, **179**
    Cranberry-Black Walnut Coffee
      Cake, 177, **177**
    Cream Cheese and Raspberry Coffee
      Cake, 44, **44**
    Double Chocolate-Orange Torte, 183
California Wild Rice Confetti Shrimp
    Salad, **118,** 119
Calzones, Cheese, 155, **155**
Caprese Pasta and Steak, 52, **53**
Cauliflower-Broccoli Casserole, 148, **148**
Champagne Punch, 15, **15**
Cheddar-Thyme Sweet Onion Dip, 11
Cheese. *See also* Cream cheese
    Bacon and Gorgonzola Cornbread
      Sliders with Chipotle Mayo, **16,** 17
    Blue Cheese Ball, 14
    Brie-Pecan Quesadillas, 20
    Cheddar-Thyme Sweet Onion Dip, 11
    Cheese Calzones, 155, **155**
    Cheese-Stuffed Jalapeños, **6,** 26
    Chèvre and Tomato Spread, 8, **9**
    Got-Extra-Zucchini Spoon Bread,
      143, **143**
    Ham and Gouda Quesadillas, 20
    Ham and Swiss Skillet, 60, **60**
    Herb Cheese-Stuffed Steaks, 97, **97**
    Lasagna, 130, **130**

Make-Ahead Chili-Cheese
  Hoagies, 131
Roma Tomato-Feta Pasta, 70, **71**
Southwestern Stuffed Pizza, 154
Swiss Chicken Bundles, 138, **138**
Triple Cheese Pasta Casserole, 142, **142**
Upside-Down Pizza Pies, 153
Veggie Chili con Queso, 127, **127**
Warm Brie, 12

Cherries
  Breakfast Popovers, 47
  Chocolate-Covered Cherry
    Cookies, 171, **171**
  Dried Cherry Scones, 45
  Triple Cherry Trifle, 182, **182**
Cherry-Cola Ham, 79, **79**
Chèvre and Tomato Spread, 8, **9**

Chicken
  Bite-Size Chicken Enchiladas, 18, **18**
  Bourbon-Molasses-Glazed Chicken
    Wings, 20, **21**
  Chicken and Saffron Orzo Salad,
    122, **122**
  Chicken and Shrimp Jambalaya, **84,** 85
  Chicken Salad with Tahini
    Dressing, 65, **65**
  Citrus Baked Chicken, 123, **123**
  Cobb Salad Wraps, 165, **165**
  Creamy Chicken and Spaghetti
    Bake, 137
  Easy Chicken Tetrazzini, 82, **83**
  Garden Chicken on a Bun, 160, **160**
  Ginger-Scented Honey-Hoisin
    Chicken Thighs with Sesame, **62,** 63
  Pasta with Chicken, Green Beans,
    and Hazelnuts, 66, **66**
  Pesto Chicken Breasts with Summer
    Squash, 64, **64**
  Polynesian Honey-Pineapple
    Chicken, 110
  Southwest Grilled Chicken, 111
  Spicy Chipotle Chicken Spears, **108,** 109
  Swiss Chicken Bundles, 138, **138**
  Tortilla Soup, 67
  Upside-Down Pizza Pies, 153
Chili, Chunky Vegetable, 75
Chili con Queso, Veggie, 127, **127**

Chocolate
  Almond-Fudge Brownies, 170
  Chocolate-Covered Cherry Cookies,
    171, **171**
  Double Chocolate-Orange Torte, 183
  Double Chocolate-Strawberry
    Pancakes, **38,** 39

Whoopie Pie Treats, 172, **173**
Choose-a-Frosting Cupcakes, 178, **179**
Chunky Vegetable Chili, 75
Citrus Baked Chicken, 123, **123**
Cobb Salad Wraps, 165, **165**

Cookies and bars
  Almond-Fudge Brownies, 170
  Butterscotch Shortbread Bars, 168, **169**
  Chocolate-Covered Cherry Cookies,
    171, **171**
  Oatmeal-Apricot Cookies, 170
  Toasted Hazelnut Bars, **166,** 168
  Whoopie Pie Treats, 172, **173**
Corned Beef Hash Patties, 58
Country Swiss Steak, 75

Cranberries
  Cranberry-Black Walnut Coffee
    Cake, 177, **177**
  Cranberry Bread Pudding, 180, **180**
  Cranberry-Pistachio Pâté, 12, **13**
  Hot Cranberry Punch, 14

Cream cheese
  Cream Cheese and Raspberry Coffee
    Cake, 44, **44**
  Cream Cheese-Pumpkin Muffins, 47
  Lemon Swirl Cream Cheese Pie,
    174, 175
  Toasted Hazelnut Bars, **166,** 168
Creamy Chicken and Spaghetti Bake, 137
Creamy Shrimp and Spinach Stew, 69, **69**

D

Deep-Dish Steak and Vegetable Pie,
  134, **135**
Desserts. *See also* Cakes; Cookies
  and bars
  Brown Sugar-Peach Ice Cream, 186, **186**
  Cranberry Bread Pudding, 180, **180**
  Home-Style Apple Bake, 181
  Lemon Swirl Cream Cheese Pie,
    174, 175
  Mini Ice Cream Cookie Cups, **184,** 185
  Orange Ice in Orange Cups, 181
  Rhubarb-Raspberry Pie, 176, **176**
  Triple Cherry Trifle, 182, **182**

Dips and spreads
  Arugula Pesto Dip, 8
  Blue Cheese Ball, 14
  Cheddar-Thyme Sweet Onion Dip, 11
  Chèvre and Tomato Spread, 8, **9**
  Cranberry-Pistachio Pâté, 12, **13**
  Fresh Onion Dip, **10,** 11
  Warm Brie, 12

Double Chocolate-Orange Torte, 183
Double Chocolate-Strawberry
  Pancakes, **38,** 39
Doughnut Muffins, 46, **46**
Dried Cherry Scones, 45

Drinks
  Champagne Punch, 15, **15**
  Hot Cranberry Punch, 14

E

Easy Chicken Tetrazzini, 82, **83**
Eggplant
  Aegean Casserole, 132
  Taverna Veggie Sandwiches, 164

Eggs
  Eggs in Purgatory with Artichoke
    Hearts, Potatoes, and Capers, **34,** 35
  French Onion Omelet, 33
  Ham and Swiss Skillet, 60, **60**
  Overnight Egg and Sausage Strata,
    32, **32**
  Popover Egg Nests, 30
  Salmon and Eggs Benedict with
    Easy Hollandaise, 31, **31**
  Zucchini and Feta Cheese Soufflés, 33

F

Fettuccine with Asparagus, 126
Fig, Wine-Braised, and Caramelized
  Onion Sandwich, Open-Faced, **162,** 163
Fish. *See* Salmon; Tuna
Flank Steak with Parsley and Lemon, 58
French Onion Omelet, 33
French Toast, No-Fry, 37, **37**
Fresh Onion Dip, **10,** 11
Fruit. *See also* specific fruits
  Minted Fruit Compote, 48
  Moroccan Lamb and Fruit Stew, 81, **81**

G

Garden Chicken on a Bun, 160, **160**
Garlic-Basil Mashed Potatoes, 149, **149**
Gingered Beef Stir-Fry, **50,** 52
Gingered Melon, 48, **49**
Ginger-Scented Honey-Hoisin
  Chicken Thighs with Sesame, **62,** 63
Go-Anywhere Baked Beans, 131
Got-Extra-Zucchini Spoon Bread, 143, **143**
Grains. *See also* Rice
  Beef-and-Barley-Stuffed Peppers,
    112, 115

Oatmeal-Apricot Cookies, 170
Orzo and Bulgur Salad, 147, **147**
Great Greek Pitas, 116, **117**
Green Beans, Chicken, and Hazelnuts,
Pasta with, 66, **66**
Greens. *See* Arugula; Lettuce; Spinach
Grilled Flank Steak and Onions, 96
Grilled Salmon with Tomato-Ginger
Relish, 104
Grilled Steak and Plum Pizzettes, **54,** 55
Grilled Tuna Sandwiches with
Rémoulade, 161, **161**

H

Ham
Cherry-Cola Ham, 79, **79**
Ham and Gouda Quesadillas, 20
Ham and Swiss Skillet, 60, **60**
Savory Ham and Rice, 116
Tuscan Ham and Bean Soup, 80, **80**
Hazelnut, Toasted, Bars, **166,** 168
Herb Cheese-Stuffed Steaks, 97, **97**
Hoisin-Sauced Turkey Tenderloin, 86, **87**
Home-Style Apple Bake, 181
Honey-Glazed Creole Pork Tenderloin
with Jambalaya Stuffing, **102,** 103
Hot Cranberry Punch, 14

I

Ice Cream, Brown Sugar-Peach, 186, **186**
Ice Cream Cookie Cups, Mini, **184,** 185
Italian Beef and Spinach Pie, 133

L

Ladder Loaf with Roasted Pepper
Filling, 19
Lamb
Mediterranean Burgers, **92,** 100
Moroccan Lamb and Fruit Stew, 81, **81**
Rosemary Lamb Chops, 59
Lasagna, 130, **130**
Layered Potatoes and Leeks, 126
Lemon Swirl Cream Cheese Pie, **174,** 175
Lentils, Seared Salmon with, 120, **120**
Lentil Sauce, Pasta with, 89
Lettuce and Teriyaki Beef Wraps, **114,** 115

M

Make-Ahead Chili-Cheese Hoagies, 131
Mango Relish, Brats with, 100, **101**
Marinated Tuna Steaks, 107
Mashed New Potatoes, 58
Meatballs
Meatball Sandwiches, 158
Mexican Meatballs, 22, **23**
Teriyaki Beef and Lettuce Wraps,
114, 115
Mediterranean Burgers, **92,** 100
Melon
Gingered Melon, 48, **49**
Melon and Salami on Rye, 159, **159**
Salami, Fruit, and Pasta Salad, 136
Mexican Meatballs, 22, **23**
Midwestern Potato Salad, 146
Mini Ice Cream Cookie Cups, **184,** 185
Minted Fruit Compote, 48
Mom's Tuna-Noodle Casserole, 139
Moroccan Lamb and Fruit Stew, 81, **81**
Muffins, Cream Cheese-Pumpkin, 47
Muffins, Doughnut, 46, **46**
Mushroom, Beef, and Onion Tart, 152, **152**
Mushroom Goulash, 88

N

No-Fry French Toast, 37, **37**
Noodles
Mom's Tuna-Noodle Casserole, 139
Mushroom Goulash, 88
Tuna-Spinach Noodle Casserole, 139
Nuts. *See also* Almonds; Pecans; Walnuts
Butterscotch Shortbread Bars, 168, **169**
Cranberry-Pistachio Pâté, 12, **13**
Toasted Hazelnut Bars, **166,** 168

O

Oatmeal-Apricot Cookies, 170
Olive and Arugula Salad Pizza, **150,** 153
Omelet, French Onion, 33
Onions
Beef, Mushroom, and Onion Tart,
152, **152**
Cheddar-Thyme Sweet Onion Dip, 11
French Onion Omelet, 33
Fresh Onion Dip, **10,** 11
Grilled Flank Steak and Onions, 96
Open-Faced Wine-Braised Fig and
Caramelized Onion Sandwich,
162, 163

Smothered Steak with Honeyed Red
Onion, 56, **56**
Vidalia Sweetest Onion-licious Pie,
24, 25
Open-Faced Wine-Braised Fig and
Caramelized Onion Sandwich, **162,** 163
Oranges
Black Bean and Orange Salad, **124,** 125
Citrus Baked Chicken, 123, **123**
Double Chocolate-Orange Torte, 183
Orange Ice in Orange Cups, 181
Orange Sticky Rolls, 40, **40**
Orzo and Bulgur Salad, 147, **147**
Overnight Egg and Sausage Strata, 32, **32**

P

Pancakes
Double Chocolate-Strawberry
Pancakes, **38,** 39
Sunrise Whole Wheat Griddle
Cakes, 36, **36**
Papaya and Pork Salad, 59
Pasta. *See also* Noodles
Aegean Casserole, 132
Caprese Pasta and Steak, 52, **53**
Chicken and Saffron Orzo Salad,
122, **122**
Creamy Chicken and Spaghetti
Bake, 137
Easy Chicken Tetrazzini, 82, **83**
Fettuccine with Asparagus, 126
Lasagna, 130, **130**
Orzo and Bulgur Salad, 147, **147**
Pasta with Broccoli and Ginger, 70
Pasta with Chicken, Green Beans,
and Hazelnuts, 66, **66**
Pasta with Lentil Sauce, 89
Pasta with Seafood, 121
Pepper Shrimp in Peanut Sauce, 68, **68**
Roma Tomato-Feta Pasta, 70, **71**
Salami, Fruit, and Pasta Salad, 136
Saucy Multigrain Spaghetti with
Tofu, 90, **91**
Spinach Pasta Salad with Lemon
Balsamic Dressing, **140,** 141
Swiss Chicken Bundles, 138, **138**
Triple Cheese Pasta Casserole, 142, **142**
Peaches
Brown Sugar-Peach Ice Cream, 186, **186**
Port-Glazed Grilled Salmon with
Basil-Peach Relish, 106, **106**
Sizzling Steak and Peaches, 94, **94**

Pecans
Brie-Pecan Quesadillas, 20
Pecan-Molasses Waffles, 41, **41**
Pecan-Praline Cinnamon Rolls, 42, 43
Peppers
Beef-and-Barley-Stuffed Peppers, **112,** 115
Cheese-Stuffed Jalapeños, **6,** 26
Ladder Loaf with Roasted Pepper Filling, 19
Pepper Shrimp in Peanut Sauce, 68, **68**
Shrimp, Roasted Red Pepper, and Prosciutto Bliss, **156,** 157
Shrimp with Sweet Pepper Relish, 107
Skirt Steak Fajitas with Grilled Onions and Peppers, 95, **95**
White Bean and Pepper Salad, 146
Pesto Chicken Breasts with Summer Squash, 64, **64**
Pies
Deep-Dish Steak and Vegetable Pie, 134, **135**
Italian Beef and Spinach Pie, 133
Lemon Swirl Cream Cheese Pie, **174,** 175
Rhubarb-Raspberry Pie, 176, **176**
Vidalia Sweetest Onion-licious Pie, **24,** 25
Pineapple-Honey Chicken, Polynesian, 110
Pistachio-Cranberry Pâté, 12, **13**
Pizza
Grilled Steak and Plum Pizzettes, **54,** 55
Olive and Arugula Salad Pizza, **150,** 153
Reuben Pizza, 154
Shrimp, Roasted Red Pepper, and Prosciutto Bliss, **156,** 157
Southwestern Stuffed Pizza, 154
Upside-Down Pizza Pies, 153
Plum and Grilled Steak Pizzettes, **54,** 55
Polynesian Honey-Pineapple Chicken, 110
Popover Egg Nests, 30
Popovers, Breakfast, 47
Pork. *See also* Bacon; Ham; Sausages
Balsamic Pork Chops, 61
Cranberry-Pistachio Pâté, 12, **13**
Great Greek Pitas, 116, **117**
Honey-Glazed Creole Pork Tenderloin with Jambalaya Stuffing, **102,** 103
Mexican Meatballs, 22, **23**
Pork and Papaya Salad, 59
Pulled Pork Sandwiches with Root Beer Barbecue Sauce, 78, **78**
Ribs with Apple and Sauerkraut, 76, **77**

Port-Glazed Grilled Salmon with Basil-Peach Relish, 106, **106**
Potatoes
Corned Beef Hash Patties, 58
Garlic-Basil Mashed Potatoes, 149, **149**
Layered Potatoes and Leeks, 126
Mashed New Potatoes, 58
Midwestern Potato Salad, 146
Summer-Style Potato Salad, 145
Pulled Pork Sandwiches with Root Beer Barbecue Sauce, 78, **78**
Pumpkin-Cream Cheese Muffins, 47

Q
Quesadillas, Brie-Pecan, 20
Quesadillas, Ham and Gouda, 20

R
Raspberry and Cream Cheese Coffee Cake, 44, **44**
Raspberry-Rhubarb Pie, 176, **176**
Reuben Pizza, 154
Rhubarb-Raspberry Pie, 176, **176**
Ribs with Apple and Sauerkraut, 76, **77**
Rice
California Wild Rice Confetti Shrimp Salad, **118,** 119
Chicken and Shrimp Jambalaya, **84,** 85
Honey-Glazed Creole Pork Tenderloin with Jambalaya Stuffing, **102,** 103
Savory Ham and Rice, 116
Tuna and Rice Casserole, 139
Roma Tomato-Feta Pasta, 70, **71**
Rosemary Lamb Chops, 59

S
Salads
Black Bean and Orange Salad, **124,** 125
California Wild Rice Confetti Shrimp Salad, **118,** 119
Chicken and Saffron Orzo Salad, 122, **122**
Chicken Salad with Tahini Dressing, 65, **65**
Midwestern Potato Salad, 146
Orzo and Bulgur Salad, 147, **147**
Pork and Papaya Salad, 59
Salami, Fruit, and Pasta Salad, 136
Spinach and Basil Salad with Beef, 57, **57**

Spinach Pasta Salad with Lemon Balsamic Dressing, **140,** 141
Summer-Style Potato Salad, 145
Warm Spinach and Scallop Salad, 67
White Bean and Pepper Salad, 146
Salami, Fruit, and Pasta Salad, 136
Salami and Melon on Rye, 159, **159**
Salmon
Grilled Salmon with Tomato-Ginger Relish, 104
Port-Glazed Grilled Salmon with Basil-Peach Relish, 106, **106**
Salmon and Eggs Benedict with Easy Hollandaise, 31, **31**
Seared Salmon with Lentils, 120, **120**
Sesame Salmon with Asian Slaw, 104, **105**
Sandwiches. *See also* Burgers
Brats with Mango Relish, 100, **101**
Cobb Salad Wraps, 165, **165**
Garden Chicken on a Bun, 160, **160**
Great Greek Pitas, 116, **117**
Grilled Tuna Sandwiches with Rémoulade, 161, **161**
Make-Ahead Chili-Cheese Hoagies, 131
Meatball Sandwiches, 158
Melon and Salami on Rye, 159, **159**
Open-Faced Wine-Braised Fig and Caramelized Onion Sandwich, **162,** 163
Pulled Pork Sandwiches with Root Beer Barbecue Sauce, 78, **78**
Speedy Pesto Wraps, 164
Taverna Veggie Sandwiches, 164
Saucy Multigrain Spaghetti with Tofu, 90, **91**
Sauerkraut
Reuben Pizza, 154
Ribs with Apple and Sauerkraut, 76, **77**
Sausages
Brats with Mango Relish, 100, **101**
Country Swiss Steak, 75
Honey-Glazed Creole Pork Tenderloin with Jambalaya Stuffing, **102,** 103
Melon and Salami on Rye, 159, **159**
Overnight Egg and Sausage Strata, 32, **32**
Salami, Fruit, and Pasta Salad, 136
Savory Ham and Rice, 116
Scallops
Pasta with Seafood, 121
Scallops in Curry Sauce, 121
Warm Spinach and Scallop Salad, 67
Scones, Blueberry Breakfast, 45
Scones, Dried Cherry, 45

Seared Salmon with Lentils, 120, **120**
Sesame Salmon with Asian Slaw, 104, **105**
Shellfish. *See also* Shrimp
    Pasta with Seafood, 121
    Scallops in Curry Sauce, 121
    Warm Spinach and Scallop Salad, 67
Shrimp
    California Wild Rice Confetti
        Shrimp Salad, **118,** 119
    Chicken and Shrimp Jambalaya, **84,** 85
    Creamy Shrimp and Spinach Stew,
        69, **69**
    Honey-Glazed Creole Pork Tenderloin
        with Jambalaya Stuffing, **102,** 103
    Pasta with Seafood, 121
    Pepper Shrimp in Peanut Sauce, 68, **68**
    Shrimp, Roasted Red Pepper, and
        Prosciutto Bliss, **156,** 157
    Shrimp with Sweet Pepper Relish, 107
    Tequila-Marinated Shrimp, 26
Sizzling Steak and Peaches, 94, **94**
Skirt Steak Fajitas with Grilled Onions
    and Peppers, 95, **95**
Smoky Barbecued Bison Burgers, 99, **99**
Smothered Steak with Honeyed Red
    Onion, 56, **56**
Soufflés, Zucchini and Feta Cheese, 33
Soups and stews. *See also* Chili
    Creamy Shrimp and Spinach Stew,
        69, **69**
    Moroccan Lamb and Fruit Stew, 81, **81**
    Tortilla Soup, 67
    Tuscan Ham and Bean Soup, 80, **80**
Southwestern Stuffed Pizza, 154
Southwest Grilled Chicken, 111
Speedy Pesto Wraps, 164
Spicy Chipotle Chicken Spears, **108,** 109
Spinach
    Cheese Calzones, 155, **155**
    Creamy Shrimp and Spinach Stew,
        69, **69**
    Italian Beef and Spinach Pie, 133
    Spinach and Basil Salad with Beef,
        57, **57**
    Spinach Pasta Salad with Lemon
        Balsamic Dressing, **140,** 141
    Warm Spinach and Scallop Salad, 67
Squash. *See also* Zucchini
    Cream Cheese-Pumpkin Muffins, 47
    Pesto Chicken Breasts with Summer
        Squash, 64, **64**
Stay-Awake Steak, 96
Strawberry-Double Chocolate
    Pancakes, **38,** 39

Summer Style Potato Salad, 145
Sunrise Whole Wheat Griddle Cakes,
    36, **36**
Swiss Chicken Bundles, 138, **138**

T

Tart, Beef, Mushroom, and Onion,
    152, **152**
Tartlets, Tomato Quiche, 22
Taverna Veggie Sandwiches, 164
Tequila-Marinated Shrimp, 26
Teriyaki Beef and Lettuce Wraps, **114,** 115
Toasted Almonds with Rosemary and
    Cayenne, 27, **27**
Toasted Hazelnut Bars, **166,** 168
Tofu, Saucy Multigrain Spaghetti with,
    90, **91**
Tomatoes
    Chèvre and Tomato Spread, 8, **9**
    Eggs in Purgatory with Artichoke
        Hearts, Potatoes, and Capers, 34, 35
    Grilled Salmon with Tomato-Ginger
        Relish, 104
    Roma Tomato-Feta Pasta, 70, **71**
    Tomato Quiche Tartlets, 22
Tortillas
    Brie-Pecan Quesadillas, 20
    Cobb Salad Wraps, 165, **165**
    Ham and Gouda Quesadillas, 20
    Skirt Steak Fajitas with Grilled
        Onions and Peppers, 95, **95**
    Speedy Pesto Wraps, 164
    Tortilla Soup, 67
    Turkey Tamale Casserole, 139
Triple Cheese Pasta Casserole, 142, **142**
Triple Cherry Trifle, 182, **182**
Tri-Tip Steaks with Texas Toast, 98, **98**
Tuna
    Grilled Tuna Sandwiches with
        Rémoulade, 161, **161**
    Marinated Tuna Steaks, 107
    Mom's Tuna-Noodle Casserole, 139
    Tuna and Rice Casserole, 139
    Tuna-Spinach Noodle Casserole, 139
Turkey
    Hoisin-Sauced Turkey Tenderloin,
        86, **87**
    Speedy Pesto Wraps, 164
    Turkey Tamale Casserole, 139
    Zesty Skillet Turkey, 61
Tuscan Ham and Bean Soup, 80, **80**

U

Upside-Down Pizza Pies, 153

V

Vegetables. *See also* specific vegetables
    Chunky Vegetable Chili, 75
    Deep-Dish Steak and Vegetable
        Pie, 134, **135**
    Garden Chicken on a Bun, 160, **160**
    Taverna Veggie Sandwiches, 164
    Veggie Chili con Queso, 127, **127**
Vidalia Sweetest Onion-licious Pie, **24,** 25

W

Waffles, Pecan-Molasses, 41, **41**
Walnuts
    Butterscotch Shortbread Bars, 168, **169**
    Cranberry-Black Walnut Coffee
        Cake, 177, **177**
Warm Brie, 12
Warm Spinach and Scallop Salad, 67
White Bean and Pepper Salad, 146
Whoopie Pie Treats, 172, **173**
Wild Rice Confetti Shrimp Salad,
    California, **118,** 119

Z

Zesty Skillet Turkey, 61
Zucchini
    Chunky Vegetable Chili, 75
    Got-Extra-Zucchini Spoon Bread,
        143, **143**
    Zucchini and Feta Cheese Soufflés, 33

Metric Information

The charts on this page provide a guide for converting measurements from the U.S. customary system, which is used throughout this book, to the metric system.

PRODUCT DIFFERENCES

Most of the ingredients called for in the recipes in this book are available in most countries. However, some are known by different names. Here are some common American ingredients and their possible counterparts:

- Sugar (white) is granulated, fine granulated, or castor sugar.
- Confectioners' sugar is icing sugar.
- All-purpose flour is enriched, bleached, or unbleached white household flour. When self-rising flour is used in place of all-purpose flour in a recipe that calls for leavening, omit the leavening agent (baking soda or baking powder) and salt.
- Light-color corn syrup is golden syrup.
- Cornstarch is cornflour.
- Baking soda is bicarbonate of soda.
- Vanilla or vanilla extract is vanilla essence.
- Green, red, or yellow sweet peppers are capsicums or bell peppers.
- Golden raisins are sultanas.

VOLUME AND WEIGHT

The United States traditionally uses cup measures for liquid and solid ingredients. The chart, top right, shows the approximate imperial and metric equivalents. If you are accustomed to weighing solid ingredients, the following approximate equivalents will be helpful.

- 1 cup butter, castor sugar, or rice = 8 ounces = ½ pound = 250 grams
- 1 cup flour = 4 ounces = ¼ pound = 125 grams
- 1 cup icing sugar = 5 ounces = 150 grams

Canadian and U.S. volume for a cup measure is 8 fluid ounces (237 ml), but the standard metric equivalent is 250 ml.

1 British imperial cup is 10 fluid ounces.

In Australia, 1 tablespoon equals 20 ml, and there are 4 teaspoons in the Australian tablespoon.

Spoon measures are used for smaller amounts of ingredients. Although the size of the tablespoon varies slightly in different countries, for practical purposes and for recipes in this book, a straight substitution is all that's necessary. Measurements made using cups or spoons always should be level unless stated otherwise.

COMMON WEIGHT RANGE REPLACEMENTS

Imperial / U.S.	Metric
½ ounce	15 g
1 ounce	25 g or 30 g
4 ounces (¼ pound)	115 g or 125 g
8 ounces (½ pound)	225 g or 250 g
16 ounces (1 pound)	450 g or 500 g
1¼ pounds	625 g
1½ pounds	750 g
2 pounds or 2¼ pounds	1,000 g or 1 Kg

OVEN TEMPERATURE EQUIVALENTS

Fahrenheit Setting	Celsius Setting*	Gas Setting
300°F	150°C	Gas Mark 2 (very low)
325°F	160°C	Gas Mark 3 (low)
350°F	180°C	Gas Mark 4 (moderate)
375°F	190°C	Gas Mark 5 (moderate)
400°F	200°C	Gas Mark 6 (hot)
425°F	220°C	Gas Mark 7 (hot)
450°F	230°C	Gas Mark 8 (very hot)
475°F	240°C	Gas Mark 9 (very hot)
500°F	260°C	Gas Mark 10 (extremely hot)
Broil	Broil	Grill

*Electric and gas ovens may be calibrated using celsius. However, for an electric oven, increase celsius setting 10 to 20 degrees when cooking above 160°C. For convection or forced air ovens (gas or electric) lower the temperature setting 25°F/10°C when cooking at all heat levels.

BAKING PAN SIZES

Imperial / U.S.	Metric
9x1½-inch round cake pan	22- or 23x4-cm (1.5 L)
9x1½-inch pie plate	22- or 23x4-cm (1 L)
8x8x2-inch square cake pan	20x5-cm (2 L)
9x9x2-inch square cake pan	22- or 23x4.5-cm (2.5 L)
11x7x1½-inch baking pan	28x17x4-cm (2 L)
2-quart rectangular baking pan	30x19x4.5-cm (3 L)
13x9x2-inch baking pan	34x22x4.5-cm (3.5 L)
15x10x1-inch jelly roll pan	40x25x2-cm
9x5x3-inch loaf pan	23x13x8-cm (2 L)
2-quart casserole	2 L

U.S. / STANDARD METRIC EQUIVALENTS

⅛ teaspoon = 0.5 ml	⅓ cup = 3 fluid ounces = 75 ml
¼ teaspoon = 1 ml	½ cup = 4 fluid ounces = 125 ml
½ teaspoon = 2 ml	⅔ cup = 5 fluid ounces = 150 ml
1 teaspoon = 5 ml	¾ cup = 6 fluid ounces = 175 ml
1 tablespoon = 15 ml	1 cup = 8 fluid ounces = 250 ml
2 tablespoons = 25 ml	2 cups = 1 pint = 500 ml
¼ cup = 2 fluid ounces = 50 ml	1 quart = 1 litre